Untwisting Twisted Relationships

Untwisting Twisted Relationships

William Backus

Author of *Telling Yourself the Truth*

and Candace Backus

BETHANY HOUSE PUBLISHERS
MINNEAPOLIS, MINNESOTA 55438
A Division of Bethany Fellowship, Inc.

Published by Bethany House Publishers
A Division of Bethany Fellowship, Inc.
6820 Auto Club Road, Minneapolis, Minnesota 55438

Printed in the United States of America

Library of Congress Cataloging-in-Publication Data

Backus, William D.
   Untwisting twisted relationships / William Backus.
      p. cm.

   1. Interpersonal conflict. 2. Attitude (Psychology)
3. Interpersonal relations. 4. Christian life—1960—   I. Title.
BF637.I48B33   1988
158'.2—dc19   88-4579
ISBN 0-87123-998-1 (pbk.)   CIP

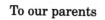

To our parents

Books by Dr. Backus

Finding the Freedom of Self-Control
Finding the Freedom of Self-Control Study Guide (with
    Steven Wiese)
The Paranoid Prophet
Telling Each Other the Truth
Telling the Truth to Troubled People
Telling Yourself the Truth (with Marie Chapian)
Telling Yourself the Truth Study Guide (with Marie Chapian)
Untwisting Twisted Relationships (with Candace Backus)
Why Do I Do What I Don't Want to Do? (with Marie
    Chapian)

Tapes by Dr. Backus

Taking Charge of Your Emotions
Telling Each Other the Truth
Telling Yourself the Truth

WILLIAM AND CANDACE BACKUS make their home in Forest Lake, Minnesota. William is a Christian psychologist and an ordained Lutheran clergyman. He is Founder and Director of the Center for Christian Psychological Services in St. Paul, Minnesota. He is also an associate pastor of a large Lutheran church. Candace is Vice President of Minnesota Psychtests, Incorporated, St. Paul, Minnesota.

The Center for Christian Psychological Services receives numerous requests for referrals to licensed Christian professional counselors who use Christian cognitive therapy as set forth in Dr. Backus' books. The Center would be happy to receive from you a brief summary of your counseling experience with misbelief therapy and your qualifications, license status, and commitment to Christian truth in your practice. On the basis of such information, the Center will refer callers from your area to you. Please include a telephone number with area code, address, and the name of the facility with which you are affiliated.

The Center for Christian Psychological Services
Roseville Professional Center #435
2233 N. Hamline
St. Paul, Minnesota, 55113
(612) 633–5290

Contents

Introduction

We've come to realize, in the context of our own relationship as husband and wife, how much people need each other.

They do, of course.

Some try to deny that they need anyone at all. Some have made it as hermits. Simeon Stylites managed to prove his grit and self-denial by living out his years at the top of a pole—alone. Others have sought apartness from mankind, living by themselves in the wilderness, thereby making the point that human needs, except for One, are not absolute.

But all who have tasted isolation have known its pain, even when they believed they had good reasons for their solitude.

Most readers of this book have felt the pain of alienation. You know the anguish of forced separation. You know how it hurts when hostility severs or interrupts, even briefly, the vital ebb and flow of a valued relationship. Some know, all too well, the cost of living perpetually in a network of anger-twisted relationships.

Some say that physical pain pales into insignificance when compared with the agony of alienation.

We believe, evidence suggests, and God's promises guarantee that the truth, which can set you, the individual, free, can also untangle your relationships. We have written this book to help you move toward freedom-transformed, truth-renewed relationships.

Please work at the tasks we have suggested. Give your relationships your best shot. Don't tell yourself it's too hard, that others need to change, not you, or that you can't do it. If you haven't much energy, use what energy you have for untwisting your relationships with the truth.

We have written this book together, pointedly in the context of our own relationships, because it is a book about relationships. We have untwisted some of the knots in our own relationship using these principles. We have tested them and found that they work. So we present them not as theories but as effective procedures, proven by us and others who have put them into practice. Now we offer them to you for untwisting your own relationships.

Much of our collaboration has taken place in the summer sunshine of our own backyard, by the winter warmth of our living room fire, and at our dining room table, for we are best friends who talk together a lot. For months we researched and discussed—yes, and put into practice—the principles we've set out here.

Together we came up with a selection of specific twists to offer as examples, knowing full well a hundred others might also be discussed. However, the patience of our readers prevents letting the book grow bigger, so please use the examples as illustrations of general principles. The procedures for untwisting relationships are the same, no matter the specifics of the particular twist.

Narratives based on clinical material have been disguised beyond recognition.

When telling our experiences, we have been inconsistent in the choice of personal pronouns. Sometimes "*I*" is used. We see no point in identifying which of *us* this pronoun refers to.

Our prayers for your relationships unite with yours, ascending effectively to the throne of God for Jesus' sake.

Candace and William Backus
Forest Lake, Minnesota
Epiphany, 1988

ONE

Twisted Relationships

Rita, the first patient of the day, confides that she doesn't want to go home for a visit because her mother will expect a hug—and Rita can't bring herself to hug her mom. Though Rita believes she genuinely loves her mother, her resentment simmers too close to the surface for such close contact. Something has been twisted in this relationship. How can Rita straighten it out?

Jeremy, a colleague, admits he's not talking to his erstwhile best friend, Dale. Both of them are competing for the position of Chief Psychologist at the same clinic. Their friendship, tangled by envious rivalry, now defies Jeremy's professional training to unravel.

Jessie enrolled in a counselor-training program, believing she *had* to cure her parents' sick relationship. Instead, she learned how deeply she had become entangled by taking inappropriate responsibility for the choices and behavior of everyone in her family. Her helpless mother's near-daily phone calls, begging Jessie to tell her how to cope with her alcoholic mate, only confirmed Jessie's lifelong misbelief that *she* was the parent of her parents. This distortion of their relationship had metamorphosed into profound depression.

"I've tried to be my mother's mother all my life because she expected me to solve her problems," Jessie confided.

"Lately I've thought I need a mother myself. I've never had one." Can Jessie set these family relationships aright without severing precious ties?

TWISTED RELATIONSHIPS AND LIFE'S MISERIES

Most of us will recognize such twists in relationships and the pain they cause. Though we expect from our relationships the sweetest moments life can offer, the brutal fact is that what parents, spouses, sweethearts, friends, associates, bosses, colleagues, and neighbors say and do can cause a large share of life's miseries. Nor can we, as Christians, pretend that non-Christians have a monopoly on relationship difficulties. Our churches are remarkable fellowships made up of some of the most loving and caring people in the world. Yet nearly always, when we come to know fellow members intimately, we discover they, too, ache inside with relationship tangles.

It's unfortunate that some Christians self-righteously declare that if only you are sufficiently spiritual and submissive, and if you are attentive to praise, Scripture reading and quiet times, your relationship difficulties will vanish. Marriages will be perfect, adolescents won't rebel, no voice will ever be raised at you in anger. In short, you can attain such a level of spirituality that your relationships will be indistinguishable from heaven itself. People who lay this burden on others don't know what they're talking about. Yes, Christians have more powerful resources for untwisting their twisted relationships—but they have no insurance policy against human difficulties.

ARE RELATIONSHIPS TOO DIFFICULT?

Relationships are difficult and demanding. All relationships, if they go on long enough, eventually call for sacrifice and self-control. Today, too many people believe they should never have to sacrifice for anything. That's why many snarl themselves into destructive relationship bondages. Others, terrified at what they have witnessed, keep clear of relationships. They withdraw into themselves for safety, but they are lonely.

Most of us want close friends, but what today goes by the name of friendship is often no more than a speaking acquaintance. We are starved for deep relationships, yet we go through life keeping others at a distance. Why? Because we also want *our* rights, *our* preeminence, *our* time, *our* control, *our* way. So we stay isolated and conflicted. We want loving relationships, but we also want *our* privacy. And we have been led to swallow a lie: that we can have it both ways. Good relationships don't come easily, so we must battle with ourselves over whether we are willing to exert energy to keep them.

It's possible to solve the dilemma by settling for superficial relationships. Some parents never get close to their children; spouses can keep an invisible wall between themselves and their mates; neighbors, church members, acquaintances can serve cool notice on others to keep their distance.

A minority of men experience closeness with anyone— their parents, siblings, wives, or friends—and they aren't even aware of what they miss. The family member most people in counseling complain about on this score is Father: "My father never talked to me"; "My father wasn't interested in me"; "I never thought my father loved me"; "My father was never home." Although clients often describe their fathers as distant, hard-to-get-to-know, it used to be that mothers were rarely described that way. Lately, however, mothers also tend to shy away from total involvement with their children. Cultural forces have driven a wedge even between mothers and their own offspring! Superficiality is a common factor in the distortion of today's family relationships.

CAN YOU UNTWIST YOUR RELATIONSHIPS?

Do troubled relationships ever get straightened out? Some do. Are counselors able to help? Yes, at times. Because two persons are involved, untwisting a twisted relationship is usually more complicated than untangling an individual's life. Nevertheless, an individual can improve a relationship with another by working on himself. To some of us, relationships are so important that unsnarling them is worth whatever effort we have to make.

This book is written for that person who wants to untangle snarled human connections and progress toward deeper, more satisfying relationships by working alone on his own relationship-twisting attitudes and behavior. Two people can work through the material together, of course, if they both want to achieve marked improvement in relationship problems.

MISBELIEFS

As you work through the chapters ahead, remember your actions toward others and your feelings and attitudes about relationships are, in psychological terms, *responses*. You probably memorized this if you took Psych 101: *responses* occur as reactions to *stimuli*. Remember? That means the basic behavior unit includes two events, a *stimulus* (event 1) and a *response* (event 2). This is basic behaviorist theory. But psychologists have learned more since the days of the early behaviorists. What's "new" in psychology happens to be very old in the Bible, as well as in some of the early philosophers. That is, the *stimuli* eliciting most *human responses* are *not* events in the environment, but events in our heads! To put it another way, we act in response, not to facts and circumstances and turns of events *outside* our skins, but to *our own beliefs* about facts, circumstances and events! As Christians have always held, what saves you is faith or belief; and what determines how you feel, think and act is what you truly believe about God, yourself, the world and events.

Although most human beings prefer blaming circumstances and other people for their feelings, attitudes and actions, both psychological and scriptural evidence argues against them. Other people don't make us feel, act and judge. We do! "As a man thinks in his heart, so is he" (Prov. 23:7).

Become acquainted with your own "self-talk," or "internal monologue," or "inner speech." This ongoing thought-stream flows through the borders of your consciousness so steadily you may hardly notice it. Yet what you send down that stream—what you tell yourself moment by moment—reflects what you *actually* believe (as distinguished from what you may formally confess or even honestly *think* you believe). The stimuli eliciting your feeling and action responses consist of the sentences in your "self-talk."

If you want to know why you feel the way you feel, act the way you act, or hold certain attitudes, ask yourself what you are telling yourself about the situation. You will discover that your feelings correspond to your beliefs as these are reflected in your ongoing thoughts or "self-talk." Thus, if your feelings are miserable or your actions deplorable, check your beliefs.

Are you believing and telling yourself the truth? Jesus promised that the truth can and will make people free! Or are you believing and telling yourself distortions and inaccuracies that are contrary to God's Word and ordinary everyday fact? We have labelled these distortions *misbeliefs.*

The point here is that misbeliefs often underlie the twists in our connections with others. These must be replaced with the truth if you want relationships as free as you can make them from hang-ups, snarls and twists.

GOD'S THREE R'S

God has always had an interest in human relationships. They have never been a matter of indifference to Him. Very early in the history of the race, He expressed this intense concern to Cain, the first murderer. Six of the Ten Commandments translate God's care for our relationships into specific relationship rules. And large chunks of Jesus' teaching spell out principles for relating to others.

God can and will deal with our relationship issues. God's action to heal relationships can be summarized as God's three R's: *Revealing, Requiring,* and *Restoring.* In the ensuing chapters, we will explore how you can participate with God in His program for renewing your life with others.

As you trust God's Spirit with your relationship issues, willing to become vulnerable to God and His action in your human relationships, He will respond with power. He will *reveal* the past roots of difficulty in primary relationships, and open your eyes to the way radical misbeliefs are now creating relationship problems. He will *require* courageous truthfulness because relationship problems are caused by our own distortions and misapprehensions. Facing this fact is often painful. And finally, He will *restore* peace, harmony, love and tremendous satisfaction to relationships now crippled because of behavior and emotions arising from root misbeliefs.

Whether you are working alone or with someone else, begin by asking God to do His work of *revealing* as you try to discover your own *radical misbeliefs*. People learn their most fundamental beliefs about relationships early in life, usually in the context of interactions with those closest to them: parents, siblings, sometimes an older relative, or a teacher. Twists in these primary relationships create misbeliefs so fundamental that they are roots. Such root misbeliefs grow up and branch out to cause problems later in life. It will be helpful for you to understand how these root misbeliefs arose in the context of your first relationships.

As you work through this book, remember, God *requires* something. No so-called "self-help" book has magic power. Having better relationships comes with God's blessing on your hard effort!

Keep in mind that God desires to *restore* harmony and

happiness in the friendships and family relationships of His people. To help you keep your eye on the true goal, the next chapter discusses the strong foundations on which good relationships are built.

TWO

How Relationship Misbeliefs Develop

Primary relationships are our first experiences of inter-acting with other people. For most of us, these earliest human interactions were with our parents. Some people refuse to examine these relationships because they see no point in dwelling on the past. Some avoid all memories of the past because they are too painful.

We believe God wants to do a work of *revealing* by opening up long-closed pathways to old memories. Twists in primary relationships "bend the twig" so to speak. Unless those early twists are straightened, the individual grows up only to recreate early interpersonal hang-ups repeatedly throughout life. Twists in our later relationships reflect what we learned from those first connections with others.

RADICAL MISBELIEFS

As a convenient label for these early-formed, bottom-layer false notions about relationships, we have invented the term *radical misbeliefs*. The word *radex* (Latin) means root. So radical misbeliefs about relationships are the roots of other misbeliefs that grow out of them and depend on them. When these root notions limit one's progress in changing misbeliefs, they must be located and torn out with the truth.

Each person's fundamental beliefs about relationships

are that person's radical relationship misbeliefs. They reoccur again and again in relationships throughout the individual's life. They form the causes of the individual's relationship-twisting behavior. They may put out branches, other misbeliefs, taking many forms as they develop in various relationships.

Because these radical misbeliefs are *foundational* infrastructures, the bottommost strata, they are often unconscious or barely conscious. Notions based on them seem self-evident. We assume they're true because they once appeared perfectly correct to us and we have never exposed them to the truth.

TREVOR'S WEAK FOUNDATION

We met Trevor and Nan during a seminar. They came to us later, wondering if we could help them understand the twists in their marital relationship. The seminar lectures had developed the truth that we talk to ourselves about our current relationships in terms of what we learned in our first human interactions. We had discussed how common it is for people to overlook the origin of their deepest beliefs about other people. Then they assume those beliefs to be true, and assume also that their self-talk reflects truth when it really consists largely of distortion and untruth developed long, long ago.

Trevor had never considered for a moment attending to his own untruths. In fact, he had never thought about the possibility! We began to realize this as he described a problem currently plaguing him and Nan, a problem that held great significance: Trevor's mother had made up her mind that he and Nan *would* arrange to visit her cousin Greta when they toured France in a few weeks. Never mind that Greta lived in Germany; they could take the time to call on Greta anyway. Mother had made that clear.

"I'm fifty-two years old, and she still runs my life!" Trevor lamented.

For her part, Nan could not hold back some very uncomplimentary judgments on Trevor's relationship with his mother. "It's true," she echoed. "And what's worse, he always does *exactly* what she wants him to. I'm tired of her butting into our lives. And I'm tired of his kowtowing to her, no matter how much it upsets our plans. And what's ridiculous is that he absolutely *never* accepts the slightest suggestion from me. I want him to make up his mind which of us he's married to."

As she talked, I knew she was right about one thing: Trevor had some decisions to make about these two important relationships.

"All his life she's told him exactly what to do," Nan continued. "And she always gets angry if he doesn't carry out her instructions to the letter."

Trevor's deepening frown showed me that his wife's talking for him was beginning to aggravate. Only when Nan paused for breath did he jump back into the conversation. "Mom thinks the commandment about honoring your parents gives her a license to run my life," he explained. "She couldn't get to first base trying to boss my father, so maybe she had to take it out on me."

Trevor described his father as a stubborn, aggressive, punitive person. Far from carrying out his wife's instructions, he went out of his way to act contrary to them, a grave difficulty for Trevor's mother, who was accustomed to giving orders.

Little Trevor had taken his father as a model. And from this parental struggle he concluded, with his child mind, that real men don't take orders from their wives. At the same time, the thought of disobeying his mother filled him with fear and guilt, for he had been taught the duty of obedience to parents without reservation. Conflicted and hating himself for being so subservient to a woman, he did as Mother wished—resentfully. Each episode of guilty, resentful, slavish conformity added to Trevor's doubt about his own masculinity.

Trevor resisted even a suggestion from Nan and made a point of *not* heeding her wisdom, though it often surpassed his own. How could he accept Nan's attempts to offer advice when, according to what he had come to believe early in life, that would only punch another hole in his already tattered self-concept?

Eventually, as we talked, both Trevor and Nan understood how Trevor had continued conforming to his mother's every whim, meanwhile treating Nan the way he wished he could handle his mother. This man was replaying in his marriage certain twists in his relationship with his parents. No wonder their marriage was under terrible stress.

We'll return to Trevor and Nan. First, it will be helpful to gain further understanding of radical misbeliefs about relationships and their impact on our present interactions with others.

WE LIVE BY BELIEFS, NOT BY EVENTS AND CIRCUMSTANCES

Why do you feel the way you feel? Why do you do the things you do? Most people have been conditioned to think of their feelings and actions as perfectly straightforward responses to *events in the environment.* Most folks assume that other people make us feel and act, and never question that assumption. They tell themselves, "If I'm angry or upset, somebody else must have caused me to feel this way." They ascribe all their reactions to circumstances: "Chocolate cake makes me overeat"; "Long sermons make me squirm"; "Interesting books make me read"; "Bargains make me spend money"; "Other people make me choose things I really don't want."

But are these commonly held ideas correct? Do our actions occur as an inevitable result of circumstances? Or could they be caused by something in us? Do our feelings suddenly come over us because environmental events create them? Did we sustain our early emotional wounds and gain our emotional response habits because others simply inflicted them upon us and caused us to have them—like wounds and scars? Or could our emotions result from thoughts inside us? Did we supply our own interpretations and evaluations of the behavior of others? And do we continue throughout life to reflect those early-devised beliefs about others?

In Chapter 1, we pointed to the fact that beliefs we call "self-talk" are the true stimuli to which our actions and emotions respond. We condition our feelings and actions in relationships by the beliefs in our own heads—thoughts consisting of our interpretation and evaluation of external events. Notice that even the *early* emotional reactions of childhood were responses to our own formulations.

So, when we ask God to reveal the wellsprings of our feelings and actions in relationships, He nudges us to examine our own *beliefs*.

Jesus often told people that their beliefs determined the way things would go for them (see Matt. 8:13; 9:20). The greatest book of wisdom ever written asserts that human behavior occurs in response to the thoughts or beliefs a person holds (see Prov. 23:7). Paul wrote to tell the Philippians he had discovered a way to feel good *no matter in what circumstances he found himself* (Phil. 4:11–12).

Cognitive psychologists have rediscovered and researched these principles, and so have echoed the scriptural teaching. The most effective therapeutic methods available today apply this discovery: What a person believes and thinks determines that person's feelings and actions.[1]

Enduring negative emotion and unwanted self-defeating behavior—including sinful attitudes and actions—occur in response to erroneous beliefs (or *misbeliefs*) that the sufferer repeats endlessly to himself. If it is true that "as a man thinketh in his heart, so is he" (Prov. 23:7), it is also true that when a person's thought-life is built upon lies and mis-

---

[1]Cf. the writings of Christian psychologist-author Larry Crabb and the writings of secular authors such as Aaron T. Beck, Gregory Emery, Albert Ellis, M. J. Mahoney, D. Meichenbaum and many others.

conceptions it will result in miserable feelings and actions that harm self or others.[2]

RADICAL MISBELIEFS AND HOW THEY ARE SHAPED

Some of the misbeliefs in our heads are *radical*. That is, they are *roots* of other beliefs, giving rise to complexes of misbeliefs that govern our relationship behavior and lead to twisted relationships throughout life. These root notions were generated early in life and in the context of our first significant relationships.

THE ROLE OF THE ADVERSARY

According to the Bible, spiritual beings, too, can suffer from twisted relationships. Evil spirits exist as real entities. By their own choice they have bent and twisted their relationship with God, their good Creator. Under Satan, their director, they now wage ceaseless warfare on God and His creation, especially the human race.

One primary target toward which their efforts are directed is the human will. They know our behavior depends upon our choices, and we make our choices, to some extent, on the basis of what we believe to be true. For that reason, deception and distortion of fact appear to be the major weapons used by these demonic enemies. Furthermore, Satan is capable of communicating with the human spirit so as to insinuate his falsehoods into our thinking. According to Jesus, Satan is the father of lies (John 8:44).

Misbeliefs, therefore, come ultimately from Satan. The early distortions in our beliefs that we are here calling *rad-*

---

[2]More detailed discussion of misbeliefs and how to find and change them for yourself can be found in the books, *Telling Yourself the Truth* by William Backus and Marie Chapian, *Telling the Truth to Troubled People,* and *Finding the Freedom of Self-Control* by William Backus, all published by Bethany House Publishers.

ical misbeliefs originated with him. To do this, he ordinarily twists our interpretations of events occurring in our earliest relationship experiences. Evidently, Satan can make use of interactions with others in these early relationships as occasions for instilling deep and influential erroneous interpretations of reality and values. He apparently is able to insinuate thoughts directly into our minds. Such mental whisperings seem to have been his method of tempting Jesus.

Perhaps this satanic influence is how some of our radical misbeliefs came to us. But the process is also more complex than that. Because we grow up in families, with parental or other primary, adult influences, we learn many of our radical misbeliefs.

One way we learn misbeliefs is by the *verbal implanting* of false notions about life and others as expressed by the primary adults in our lives. Clients in our clinic uncover these misbeliefs, planted early in their spirits with the power of the parental voice. The misbeliefs continue into their own adulthood. For instance, Jerry, who believed it was dangerous to have close friends, recalled how his mother, frustrated at some of *her* friends, had once let her emotions get the better of her. "Jerry, don't ever make a friend; they stab you in the back!" she shouted at her little boy, without the slightest suspicion that he would take her angry tirade to heart and with it twist all his relationships! In this example, Satan rode on the thoughtless, emotional outburst of the boy's mother to implant the falsehood. The notion became one of his *radical misbeliefs*!

Other misbeliefs which can be learned from adult verbalization include: "Religious people are weak"; "Religion is for women and old people"; "Only sissies show their feelings"; "Women (or men) are stupid." No doubt you can add some of your own misbeliefs to this list. Regarding satanic influence, the Evil One takes these expressions and causes the child to use them to explain the world of relationships for himself—to the detriment of his own precious relationships.

Another way the adults in our early relationships held influence was in their *modeling*. Countless experiments demonstrate that children observing another person's behavior will copy that behavior, especially if the child has reason to believe the other person benefits from the behavior. Though we are not quite ready to get back to Trevor's story, we can say that he was copying his father's irrational avoidance of his wife's suggestions. Trevor, quite naturally, took his father as a model.

Modeling by parents who *think* they are doing "the right thing" but who are operating from their own system of misbeliefs also has powerful effects. A child who grows up in a home where the parents never show anger or argue, for instance, may not be so fortunate as some might think. Because the child never sees conflict *resolution* modeled, he never learns how to resolve conflicts in his relationships properly. Most of these children view any conflict with another person as a terrible thing, and they will avoid conflict at almost any cost.

HYPOTHESIS CREATION

Whether a child hears misbeliefs expressed verbally or sees them modeled by adults, he must actively employ these constructions in his own interpretations of reality. So we need to know about a third device through which a child can develop misbeliefs. We can call it *hypothesis creation*.

The growing child behaves much like a scientist. The scientist observes some events. Then he wants to explain those events, so he creates a theory or hypothesis that he thinks might work out in practice. Next, he tests his hypothesis by running an experiment. If his theory seems to work in the experiment, he may then *believe* it. If it doesn't work, he forgets about it, amends it, or tries another experiment.

For example, a child who is abused or neglected may think he will get some much-needed, ego-strengthening attention if he pulls off some pranks in school. His pranks, though disruptive, make him the center of attention. Other children may welcome the pranks with envious, amused enthusiasm. To the attention-starved child this is very rewarding. Even though the child may have to report to the principal and may later be punished at home, his experiment is a "success." It confirms his hypothesis that the way to be important is to make a show of disrupting the normal flow of events. Though the desired attention comes repeatedly, the device twists the child's relationships.

If this child's radical misbelief follows him through life, it will cause him considerable trouble. Radical misbeliefs, originated by Satan, acquired through hearing them verbalized, copying a model and hypothesis-testing will twist subsequent relationships *even if the person does not realize their presence in his thoughts*.

DISCOVERING RADICAL MISBELIEFS

For clients with certain difficulties, we have found in clinical experiments that simply attending to one's stream of conscious thoughts, noticing the obvious misbeliefs about God, oneself, events, and other people, then correcting these misbeliefs with truth derived from Scripture, reason, or experience results in freedom. A simple, brief, successful procedure. For this reason, it once appeared unnecessary to rummage around in the storage bin of old memories.

But over the years, we have noted that some clients, particularly some with relationship problems, need to do more. For these clients there appear to be significant radical misbeliefs embedded in early experiences, undergirding a superstructure of misbeliefs.

Radical misbeliefs make up a strongly held creed or system of beliefs about relationships. For each person, this creed is like a distorting lens through which he views all the relationships of his life—past, present, or future. Remember, this lens of misbeliefs consists of childish thinking that has never been corrected. Some are barely available to consciousness, or they are buried in the unconscious. Often they can be recollected during a careful exploration of the past. Then, reviewed under the light of God's truth—if one wants to change them and is willing to make the effort—they can be altered with the truth. Finally, the more recent growth of relationship misbeliefs can be attacked with truth, with increased freedom in relationships as the outcome.

RADICAL MISBELIEFS IN TREVOR'S RELATIONSHIP CREED

Now let's return to Trevor to examine some of the radical misbeliefs in his relationship belief system or creed:

- I must never again allow a woman to tell me what do;
- If I accept even one suggestion from any woman, I will find I am totally controlled;
- Men who allow women to tell them what to do are weak, spineless jellyfish, losers and nonentities.

Other radical misbeliefs in Trevor's relationship creed taught him that he must carry out his mother's wishes indiscriminately, or else he would writhe with guilt; that he would never win because of his "double bind"; that he was and always would be an inferior shrimp next to his father; that his father had been free to exercise the prerogatives of a "real man," doing his own thing without a second thought; and that Trevor himself would never have this freedom.

No wonder Trevor wouldn't—*couldn't*—listen to Nan's advice! By brainwashing himself with his radical relationship misbeliefs, Trevor was doing his part to strangle his marriage.

Trevor also viewed other people's relationships through the lens of his own early-acquired radical misbeliefs. Listen to his self-talk regarding one of his professional associates.

Randy's a worm—nothing but a spineless worm.
He has to check everything with Priscilla. What a rot-

*ten excuse for a man. He won't be able to stand up to
life. When things get rough, he'll fall apart. I can't ever
let myself get weak like that!*

Predictably, Trevor's relationship with Randy remained
superficially friendly, but—in company with his other
"friendships"—it had no chance of becoming open, honest
and intimate.

PATTERNS OF TWISTED RELATIONSHIPS

Like Trevor, nearly all of us harbor radical relationship
misbeliefs. They condition and limit our marriages, friendships and family interactions.

Some of the patterns occur so often they are familiar. We
can all recognize the shapes stamped by certain radical
misbeliefs on pairs and groups of people we've known.

THE FLAWLESS HOUSEHOLD

One radical imperative in some families is this: *keep
everything smooth*. Whatever it costs, preserve the calm! We
must maintain the *sshh'd*, laid-back atmosphere of "The
Perfect Home." It is awful if anything comes askew. Quickly,
unobtrusively, put it back and perhaps no one will notice.
Noise is ugly and disruptive. "It" is not permitted—whatever
"it" is. Dad will be home soon, so the children must be
bathed, dressed, and mounted in order on the sofa to receive
him. The furniture? It's in place. The supper? Ready. The
background music? Soft, almost unnoticed, just right. Everything? Smooooth!

A moment's thought should enable you to deduce some
of the radical misbeliefs activating relationships in that
"flawless" household.

"REAL BIG GUYS" AND "REAL LITTLE GALS"

Another theme prevailing in some marriages and seep-
.o the belief systems of entire families is this one: *I'm*

the man and you're the woman and let's not get it mixed up!
He never does a dish or makes a bed; she never writes a
check or earns money.

The children are taught to believe it is terrible if males
allow feelings to show through their "manly" stoicism, or
fail to stand prepared to beat somebody up. No reinforcement
comes to boys who show interest in tenderness or pursue
quiet activities. God is supposed to have roped those off as
the proper preserve of girls.

These homes also drill into their children strange notions
about girls: Girls must always exhibit helplessness, especially around males over against whom they are to function
as passive reactors. Nature has been violated if a girl wants
to play football, or study mathematics which, it is believed,
God created specifically as men's pursuits.

I am not underestimating the importance of acquiring
appropriate sex role behaviors. I am trying to show the ab-
surdity of rigid, unscriptural misbeliefs about these behaviors.

THE STEREOTYPIC MALE HAS TROUBLE WITH
RELATIONSHIPS

Though there is nothing stereotyped about biblical de-
lineations of male or female behavior, Christians sometimes
foster cookie-cutter profiles of the sexes.

One radical misbelief so common it pervades our culture
is that of the stereotypic male: *I don't need anybody!* Because
nearly all men have been dosed with this nonsensical notion,
they often reflect it in their most characteristic behaviors.
Unless something changes, many men plod through life
without intimate relationships, not even able to grasp what
their wives are complaining about when they beg for communication. They simply don't know what they're missing
without an intervention of the truth.

In future chapters, we will study in depth some common
twisted relationship patterns like those described here. As

we work through each, we will search for underlying radical misbeliefs and replace them with the truth. It is this replacing of radical misbeliefs with truth that facilitates the work of untwisting twisted relationships.

THREE

Some "Agreed" Patterns in Twisted Relationships

When people relate to one another, they do so by agreement. True, there's nothing in writing. In fact, we never talk about the terms of these "contracts." It's surprising how many of the ordinary rules most of us agree on.

For example, in most of our relationships we assume an agreement not to hit each other. Where that basic rule is violated, the relationship may not survive. Most of these tacit contracts include a rule against sexual intercourse with the other person. Again, though this rule is almost never spelled out, violation brings serious consequences. In everyday relationships, the rules we never so much as mention prohibit either person addressing the other like a drill sergeant; we can't express our requests as peremptory commands. So many such rules govern our relationships we seldom notice them. But we obey them strictly. Many times every day, we conform to these little contracts without giving them a thought.

And though our unspoken rules ordinarily work pretty well, people do at times assume different rules. Conflict results when two people understand their unverbalized contract differently.

WHEN ASSUMED AGREEMENTS ARE MISBELIEFS

The few rules we've seen so far apply to most relationships. But other stipulations are more specific to the particular relationships in which they occur. The receptionists in my office assume I may give them orders. But my next-door neighbor knows of no such rule in our relationship contract. I may hug fellow members of my church. I may not casually hug my butcher.

Sometimes, one person in a relationship assumes certain stipulations while the other does not. Jerry assumes that when he and Cassie are married she will take his last name. Cassie assumes he won't mind if she continues to use her family surname. Kurt assumes that, because he and Mickey are best friends, Mickey won't let anything interfere with their weekly golf game. Mickey assumes that, because they are friends, Kurt will understand if he can't golf for several weeks because of an unusually burdensome workload.

Notice that when agreement does not exist between two people in a relationship, the *assumption* of agreement is a misbelief. Jerry, Cassie, Kurt and Mickey all made erroneous assumptions; they all misbelieved.

You may find that some of your relationships are characterized by your assumed rules. Do any of these sound familiar?

- He should ask me what I want to do once in a while.
- She likes it when I come in and stay for a couple of hours after our dates.
- If they don't spend at least $25 on our Christmas present, they are insulting us.
- Naturally my parents' home is always open to me, even though I am an adult and have my own family—so we can visit unannounced whenever we feel like it.

If the other parties involved do not hold these assumptions, they are your misbeliefs.

Such misbeliefs, held without any discussion or express agreement, exist in the mind of only one person. They most often follow from old radical relationship misbeliefs; they usually result in trouble. More about such relationship twists later.

SHARED MISBELIEFS ARE MISBELIEFS STILL!

More often than not, the persons in a relationship manage to complement each other's relationship misbeliefs. Their rules seem to fit each other, and perhaps that is one reason relationships develop. Therefore, you may find that some of your relationships, though they are based on agreed rules, are twisted nonetheless. This can happen if the rules are not congruent with reality or are untruthful, though both you and the other person gladly endorse them. If an agreed-upon rule is fashioned out of radical misbeliefs, it will eventually lead to a twisted relationship.

Such complementary radical relationship misbeliefs might actually bring two people together. Blind to the attractive power of mutually-fitting radical misbeliefs, they imagine they were made *for* each other, when they were really shaped *like* each other, or were bent to conform to each other. They can make a contract because their twisted radical misbeliefs readily twist together. Trouble comes when, in spite of shared radical misbeliefs, the individuals find that the other holds assumptions which conflict.

Some twisted relationship patterns are common. We can recognize and label them because we've seen them or have even been involved in them. But each pairing will have its own individuality, ringing unique changes on the standard pattern, for in such a relationship the participants will hold conflicting radical misbeliefs in addition to the radical misbelief they both hold in common.

HELEN AND GARY

Helen sees Gary as a poor, helpless man who needs a mother. This tugs at her strong need to nurture somebody until the pull becomes irresistible. Gary may detect a nurturing person in Helen. So Gary's strong wish for succor and caring draws him to Helen as magnetic north to south. But neither Helen nor Gary realizes his own or the other's misbeliefs, nor do they suspect the covert operation of hidden assumptions.

But those hidden assumptions drive behavior! So Helen assumes she has a God-given right to tell Gary what to do since she takes such good care of him. Gary assumes that Helen's tender care is his due, no strings attached, solely because he is valuable and lovable. Accordingly, Gary recognizes no obligation to put up with what he thinks of as Helen's unremitting nagging. Inwardly, each repeats his false assumptions as if they were true. They thus stay unhappy and angry with each other.

Notice the assorted erroneous assumptions. In fact, get in the habit of spelling out the radical misbeliefs you detect in relationship patterns. For instance, Helen learned early in life to believe: *I am worthwhile only when I am proving my value by taking care of some helpless, passive male.* Gary, on the other hand, learned in his primary relationship context to believe: *If someone loves me, she will take care of me, wait on me, and work for me for no other reason than that I am so cute and lovable.* It won't work, because eventually Helen will expect more from Gary than merely being desirable.

PYRAMIS AND THISBEE

Though Pyramis and Thisbee are fictional characters, I find in their relationship, nonetheless, another common pattern, twisted by complementary erroneous radical misbeliefs. See if you recognize real people in this famous scenario.

Pyramis was raised in a family where love came to mean allowing yourself to be manipulated by guilt feelings. He found himself inexplicably attracted to Thisbee, who had learned to be silent and tearful when she was angry. During such protracted periods, guilt-prone Pyramis waxed ever more solicitous, attentive and loving. So they twined together in a pattern of choking anguish that neither understood. The twist here is self-perpetuating, and the unresolved, intensifying anger ultimately destroys the relationship.

You may recognize that Pyramis had acquired this radical misbelief: *Unless you live up to the other person's every expectation, you are supposed to feel terrible until she lets you off the hook.* Thisbee had learned from her father's modeling that *angry or disappointed feelings are expressed by dignified silence, with manifestations of hurt uncontrollable.*

DETECT YOUR OWN SHARED OR COMPLEMENTARY MISBELIEFS

Presently, you will read about other common twist patterns in relationships. As you read, you may identify patterns in your own relationships, discovering radical misbeliefs of which you were unaware. Or you may learn how to detect and expose your own peculiar radical misbeliefs. You will want to pay special attention to the way these warp your own significant involvements with other human beings.

Just before we examine these misbeliefs, I want to give a word of caution having to do with *blame.*

It is unpleasant to face and admit twists in ourselves, our loved ones, or our connections with others—especially when the twists manifest themselves primarily in relationships. Our first thought is to find fault with someone else and avoid the embarrassing conclusion that we may not be perfect. So, the sinful human response is to blame someone else. When God called Adam to account for his disobedience, Adam immediately resorted to blame: He blamed God and his wife, Eve. When the Lord turned to Eve, she blamed the serpent. So mankind was off and running on the blame track.

We all experience the powerful urge to blame. We will

blame even those we say we love most—mother, father, sister, brother, wife, husband, friend, child—anyone but ourselves. Watch for this misbelief in yourself: *It's vital to blame someone. That's the only way I can make myself righteous.* What a lie! In the first place, blaming is ineffective and untruthful and, even more important, you can't make yourself right by doing it. There is only one way to be right: God's way.

God's righteousness is Jesus Christ. We can be genuinely righteous only by accepting God's forgiveness as a gracious gift, offered because Jesus suffered the penalty of our unrighteousness when He shed His blood and died on the cross. By letting God cover your sin with Jesus' righteousness, you can rid yourself of the irrational need to blame someone, *anyone,* to make yourself look good. You can accept and frankly acknowledge your own sinful actions and their related radical misbeliefs. You can admit the significant role of your own behavior in twisting your relationships.

Many people do not differentiate between blaming and understanding causes when it comes to analyzing their radical misbeliefs. I may recognize that I learned a misbelief through a twisted relationship with my mother, for example, without blaming and criticizing her for her role. I can tell myself the truth: She did the very best she could but, being human, was herself subject to the warping effects of sin and the limitations of human finiteness. I must not expect perfect performance from others any more than from myself. But I can, without rancor, trace the parts I and others have played in the formation of my beliefs and misbeliefs.

This we will now begin to do.

FOUR

The Radical Misbeliefs of Loneliness

These days loneliness is an epidemic! What pain it has brought to enormous numbers of alienated, aching human beings!

Perhaps you think of loneliness as the lack of satisfying relationships with other people, caused by factors that are out of your control. There is much more to loneliness than that, however. It has its roots in radical misbeliefs, for it is actually a thicket of truly twisted relationships. The chronically lonely individual has little else but twisted relationships with everyone, including himself.

WHAT LONELINESS IS

What *is* loneliness? Is it merely being alone? No, for the lonely often feel most alone in the midst of a crowd. People become mere faces, not persons we know and love.

The conditions of our life today make it especially easy for people to become lonely. Though we may live jammed into the same building, we ignore one another. We work side-by-side, but when we meet on the street, we exchange no greeting. Most of our mail comes from machines that transfer our names automatically from long, impersonal lists to long, impersonal envelopes stuffed with "personalized" impersonal appeals for patronage or gifts.

Yes, we can be surrounded by people, hounded by their ceaseless automated attention, or crowded up close against their bodies in the smallest spaces. Yet we can suffer the sharp agony of loneliness.

Loneliness is not being alone, and aloneness need not be lonely. Solitude can soothe the mind and quiet the soul. We need time apart to find what Jesus discovered: the presence of God. Because He craved solitude, Jesus went alone to the desert, or climbed a mountain. He kept vigil through the night because then all the world slept. To Him, aloneness meant, not abandonment by others, but communion with the Father.

It will not do, then, to think of loneliness as merely being by oneself. To understand it better, let's look at a portrait of the lonely person.

A COMPOSITE PICTURE OF THE LONELY PERSON

Jeffrey E. Young, a therapist with considerable experience in helping lonely clients, has developed a composite picture of the lonely person.[1]

Lonely people have nobody they can depend upon to care for them. Nobody in their lives understands them. Day after day they exist with no opportunity to share their secret feelings with any human being. They belong to no group of friends and feel a part of no human enterprise. Nobody they know needs or wants them, nobody covets their love. Sharing values, dreams and interests with other people has no place in their lives, and there is no one with whom to enjoy good moments. Even at work their relationships are not warm and sharing, as among equals. They have no friends they feel they can trust.

Lonely people think often about their losses: friends now gone who cannot be replaced; the emptiness of their hearts;

---

[1]Jeffrey E. Young, *Cognitive Therapy and Loneliness*, in *New Directions in Cognitive Therapy*, Eds., John P. Foreyt and Diana P. Rathjen (New York: Plenum Press, 1978).

their yearning for intimacy. Sometimes lonely people are married, but closeness is lacking nevertheless. Although lonely singles often envy those who are married, marriage is no automatic remedy. Many who are married suffer from acute loneliness. And most of us would not want the meager, distant relationships lonely people have, for they do not satisfy.

LONELY, MISBELIEVING BETTY

Betty, a shy woman of twenty-seven, came to our clinic for help with depression, which had endured for most of her adult life and perhaps longer. "I don't have anything to live for," she said. "I'm so lonely." Betty's misery was no biochemical disorder, no freak of chance. It was the fruit of real, honest-to-goodness loneliness. The life Betty described was composed of office work (to earn her living) and TV watching (to kill time).

Betty, and others suffering from loneliness, easily identify with the psalmist, who wrote:

> Be gracious to me, O Lord, for I am in distress, and my eyes are dimmed with grief. . . . Strong as I am, I stumble under my load of misery. . . . My neighbours find me a burden, my friends shudder at me; when they see me in the street they turn quickly away. I am forgotten, like a dead man out of mind; I have come to be like something lost. (Ps. 31:9–12, The New English Bible)

"I just don't understand," Betty explained, after her initial complaint about her painful loneliness. "Why does God want me to go on this way, day after day, year after year? Can't God see how I hurt?"

Although God may sometimes want us to be *alone*, He didn't create us for loneliness. "It is not good for the man to be alone," He declared as He went to work to cure Adam's loneliness. (See Genesis 2.) And God's Word exhibits some remarkable examples of close friendships.

David, the greatest king of Israel, the man after God's

own heart, had a model friendship with Jonathan. These two men were closer than breathing and loved each other dearly. Jesus, though He loved all His disciples, enjoyed a particularly close and loving companionship with His friend John.

Our potential for special closeness with one or two other Christians lies in the fact that we are all one body, according to the teachings of the Apostle Paul. We are already joined to one another by being joined to Jesus. This organic unity with every other Christian furnishes a solid basis for the development of deep-running friendships among Christians who discover that they are especially attracted to one another.

WHY ARE LONELY PEOPLE LONELY?

God didn't design our lives for loneliness; then, maybe we're lonely because we just don't have what it takes to interest anybody else in us. Aren't people lonely because they are unlikable, ugly, dull and boring? Aren't people who have no friends usually so unattractive nobody wants them?

No way! Loneliness results not from our ugliness but from our misbeliefs. The lonely person is lonely *because he lets his anxieties control his interpersonal behavior to the point where he refuses to work at forming friendships.*

When I suggested to Betty that her loneliness resulted from avoiding others, or at least not taking any initiative, she replied, "But I'm afraid."

I pointed out a misbelief: "Because you believe you must not do things you are terribly afraid of, you keep on avoiding the behaviors necessary for the formation of close relationships. Your misbeliefs cause you to perpetuate your loneliness."

Betty was surprised at the idea that her loneliness began with her beliefs. She thought loneliness was caused by circumstances beyond her control. She believed the remedy was out of her hands, the responsibility of other people, or God. Betty was waiting for other people to change her life by making friendly overtures to her.

Why do we keep believing our loneliness is some sort of curse wished upon us by a cruel God? If a lonely person will learn to combat and replace the misbeliefs leading to loneliness with truth leading to closeness, he can learn to form close friendships.

If you wish to gain self-control to diminish the amount of loneliness you feel, you will need to make some decisive changes in your own habits. To be exact, you will have to change your *misbeliefs* and *actions* in respect to relationships.

Kent's story will show you how one man did it.

KENT

His shoulders slumped and his walk had the shuffle of a man profoundly discouraged. Kent, twenty-five years old, single and forty pounds too bulky, sat facing me. More accurately, he stared at the floor.

He forced the words out, as if talking were too great a load to be borne. "I don't know what I'm doing here. I have nothing to live for. Every day I go to work, come home, go to bed. Then I get up, go to work, come home, go to bed—over and over with no point or purpose. I don't even have a girl."

"Why not?" I asked innocently.

He huffed. "What girl would want me? Look at me. I'm no movie star. And look at this gut. Who wants to go out with that?"

I could predict the direction of the conversation from this point on. I would ask him if he was working on getting a girl. He would laugh cynically and tell me he didn't need to be rejected. No, he never asked anyone out. No, he wasn't making an effort. Rejection would be too painful. He couldn't stand it.

My prediction was accurate. He made each of those points. How many countless, lonely people have I listened to as they advanced the very same arguments? And the arguments never carry any weight, based as they are on erroneous convictions.

Look at Kent's convictions yourself and I believe you'll see what I mean. Kent had insisted he was miserable enough to kill himself—but was not miserable enough to risk trying to initiate a relationship with a woman. Did he really buy the notion that he was better off killing himself than suffering anxiety or rejection? You can see how full of holes such a belief system is. Yet it kept Kent wretched and paralyzed.

Kent's most obvious and omnipresent misbelief, which he held in common with most other lonely people, was this: *I can't stand rejections.* As long as he believed that, he remained frozen in a state of inaction. As a result, Kent kept himself safe by keeping his distance from the possibility of rejection. His dominant relationship pattern, then, might be labeled, *Playing It Safe.*

THE MAJOR MISBELIEF OF THE LONELY

I have concluded, from clinical experience, that the major radical misbelief of the lonely is that *rejection is intolerable.* "Why, if I should try to make a friend, really *try*," these folks say, "it would wipe me out to fail and be rejected. I couldn't stand it. I'd be devastated!"

"Tell me exactly what it is about rejection that's so terrible?" I asked Kent. I was after hard facts, specifics. "Have you been rejected lately?"

He drummed on the desk a second or two while he thought about it. "No, I guess I haven't. Not lately. Not that I can recall right now."

"When can you remember being rejected?"

"You mean ever?"

"Ever."

Kent thought for a long time. He finally recalled a couple of very ambiguous experiences during adolescence. They *might* have been rejections by others, but Kent had reached out so gingerly and backed off so quickly when he hadn't encountered great enthusiasm at his overtures that they might *not* have been rejections at all. Almost certainly these cautious attempts had been unsuccessful because Kent was playing it safe rather than showing interest in others. In the final analysis, Kent couldn't recall one single experience of actual certified and sealed rejection.

The story is the same with many who are lonely. Terrified of rejection, they have never really been rejected. Or perhaps they have rarely experienced any other negative reactions than mild lack of interest on the part of others. I have found that most lonely people have suffered true rejection in one or more of their primary relationships, then buried these painful memories and subsequently acted on their radical misbelief. So careful have they been to avoid rejection that they haven't experienced real rejection since childhood.

Many readers are in the same boat as Kent. Your one relationship rule is, *play it safe,* and you haven't ever questioned what happened to make you so cautious. Others will be able to recall early traumatic rejection experiences in which they learned their radical misbelief about rejection.

HOW RADICAL REJECTION MISBELIEFS ARE LEARNED

Why is it that people like Kent believe rejection is so terrible they can't afford to risk it, while others take rejections in stride, not enjoying them exactly, but knowing for certain that rejection won't kill them? Why do some people play it safe to the extent that they avoid trying to have significant connections with others?

Remember, our radical misbeliefs are hammered out on the forge of primary relationships. After much prayer and conversation, during which the Spirit of God joined with Kent's spirit to search through some of his recollections from early life, we pieced together the long-overlooked and forgotten story.

Kent's father had been an alcoholic, a quiet man who rarely became upset or angry at his family. He regularly earned their daily bread, and did his drinking predictably— every evening after work at a bar within walking distance of home. Interestingly, Kent's *mother* had drawn him into the sick world of the alcoholic family by drilling into him the importance of hiding his father's problem from the whole world. It was shameful for the family to have such a difficulty, and Kent learned to say nothing to anyone. He played his part in the family cover-up. Since his mother worked evenings, it fell to Kent to get his stumbling-drunk, loudly singing father into the house and into bed quickly so the neighbors wouldn't hear his loud, raucous singing.

Kent felt deep pain throughout his childhood years, for children believe they are entitled to their parents' unlimited commitments and love. When these are not forthcoming, they try to do something to relieve their misery. In vain, the boy fought to win attention and love from his preoccupied parents. Kent's father remained distant and usually intoxicated, while his mother put all her attention into her efforts to adjust the whole world to her husband's problem. Kent was left with the resources of a little boy's thoughts to fall back on. Some time between ages five and eight, Kent determined to try for his father's love and/or his mother's interest and attention. He would be especially good! He tried redoubling his efforts and tenderness with his drunken father as he dragged the big man into bed—but his father only sank into intoxicated oblivion. He worked to become an A-student and brought his outstanding grades to his mother, only to be exhorted to try harder. His best efforts achieved nothing. So Kent began to believe there must be something wrong with *him* that would forever doom him to fail in relationships.

Kent was learning about life—but he was learning it in a twisted way. So his conclusions went like this: "No matter what I do or how hard I try, I just don't have what it takes to make others like me or want me around." Facing this belief while his parents ignored him caused anguish. Eventually Kent found he felt better if he didn't try. So he made another conclusion: "I can avoid being hurt if I don't reach out." Putting his struggle out of his thoughts, Kent continued through life, carefully avoiding any efforts to win friendship. Very deeply, he believed that such efforts could only bring him incredible agony. In this way, Kent formulated his own radical misbelief about relationships, and so assured his own loneliness.

AVOIDANCE BEHAVIOR

Why do those who fear rejection most know the least about it? Because they avoid it most assiduously. Loneliness is usually the result of what psychologists call *avoidance behavior.*

So far, we have heard how Kent became convinced that rejection was terrible and that he was bound to be rejected whenever he tried to reach out to others. We learned how he devised his radical relationship misbelief. Kent's story is unique, but elements in it are common to many others.

Here's the rest of the story for people like Kent: Once they become convinced that some experience or some object is so terrible they dare not go near it, that experience or object acquires power to elicit feelings of dread. The closer they approach to the dreaded thing, the more powerful their feelings of fear. Very quickly, they learn that by staying far away from the feared experience, they can keep themselves relatively free from dread. If they can avoid thinking about it, so much the better. So by avoiding every reminder of the frightening thing, they manage to avoid the pain it causes as well.

For the lonely, the most feared experience is rejection by any person they might reach out to befriend. So in addition to believing that *rejection is terrible,* and that *they couldn't possibly stand it,* they are convinced *they must therefore avoid rejection no matter what it takes.*

The rest follows logically. Lonely people avoid initiating friendships because they believe they leave themselves exposed to rejection, the most terrible event they can imagine. By avoidance they are protecting themselves from an experience they believe, falsely, they couldn't stand.

One typical but unforeseen result of this pattern of avoidance is that the person playing it safe never learns that the thing he or she fears so intensely is really not lethal at all. If the person with flight phobia never travels by air, he will continue to fear and to believe that the minute a plane with him aboard takes off it will crash. And if you never get yourself into a situation where you could be rejected, you will likely remain forever terrified by the very idea, perpetuating and validating the false interpretations of reality that were the best your child mind could make of things way back then.

Many lonely people have protected themselves so much from the pain of rejection that they don't experience it. They avoid reaching out to others so they cannot get their hands slapped. The result is that they never learn from experience the truth about rejection. They never have their childish misbeliefs corrected by later experience and more valid adult interpretations.

THE TRUTH ABOUT REJECTION

Most people have found they *can* stand rejections. While never pleasant, it will not even hurt very much—once you can tell yourself the truth about it.

Most people are "rejected" fairly often. That's because anyone who reaches out to others will find that some do not reciprocate. By discovering what rejection actually feels like, anyone can learn to tolerate it occasionally for the sake of the benefits to be gained by initiating relationships with others.

The truth about rejection, which most people acquire from experience, is this:

Rejection is not pleasant, but it is not terrible either, and it can't kill me.

Moreover,

Rejection is not a rare experience. Most people experience it in one form or another rather often during their lives. They handle it, they survive—and so can I.

Therefore,

The radical misbelief, I must never reach out because I couldn't stand rejection, *is false. I formulated it in the long-gone days of childhood, and it can be unlearned by having new experiences in successful relationships. It makes sense to reach out to others, to initiate friendships and, meanwhile, prepare myself to handle whatever rejections I may experience.*

As lonely people work on developing social skills and quit avoiding anxiety, they will need to tell themselves over and over the truths that rejection can be tolerated, that it happens fairly often and that avoiding rejection—though it seemed reasonable once—no longer makes any sense at all.

WHAT REJECTION DOES NOT MEAN

Still not ready to buy the notion that rejection isn't all that awful? Many lonely people dread rejection because they have never understood what rejection really means and what it *doesn't* mean. They think rejection proves that they are worthless, uninteresting and unlovable. Kent believed that rejection by anyone meant that he was undesirable and unpleasant to be with.

How do lonely people typically interpret rejection? They take it as self-evident that if others don't respond when they reach out, it is due to some undesirable quality they have:

- "It's because I'm ugly."
- "It's because I'm so serious."

- "It's because I'm too fat."
- "It's because I'm too. . . ."

These are the kinds of reflex interpretations of rejection people often give themselves. And because they assume that rejection is *always* due to some undesirable quality in them, they find rejection so terrible they can't stand it.

Most people have added additional and related misbeliefs to the radical misbelief planted in childhood. Thus another rejection misbelief common among the lonely goes like this:

> *If I reach out to another person and that person doesn't respond positively, it* proves *I'm ugly, dull, boring, and undesirable.*

Look at this common assumption for a moment. While it's true that sometimes another person will simply not consider you suitable for a friendship because of some trait of yours, it's by no means the most frequent reason for rejection. Even if someone rejects your overtures on this basis, however, you don't have to take it as a confirmation of your inferiority. Even if someone else actually believed you were "beneath" them or found you dull and uninteresting, you would not have to accept their conclusion as objective and factual. Instead, you could take it that the two of you, for now anyway, are incompatible and the friendship wouldn't work out. In fact, you can be happy to have discovered that now, at the beginning, rather than later, after you've worked hard for a relationship that's not going anywhere.

It is extremely rare for most people to reject a friendly approach by saying, "I don't like you," or "I find you too unexciting for me." Far more common reasons for not responding to someone else's overtures are traits or situational factors in the life of the person doing the rejection.

Consider: That person you've tried to reach may be one who fears closeness and avoids responding enthusiastically to anybody. Or, the other person may have no interest in developing an additional relationship at the moment and may feel that life is already too full of things to do. Occasionally, another person to whom you reach out may actually believe you are too *good* rather than too *bad*, too *intelligent*, too *devout,* too *spiritual,* or too *sophisticated* to really be interested in him or her and may therefore reject you rather than be rejected later by you. Sounds strange? As a counselor, I assure you, it happens more often than you may realize.

The point is that you must be sick and tired of your old loneliness-creating misbeliefs. You must be absolutely fed up with hearing yourself tell yourself, "You are just a dope and nobody will ever like you; you're better off to face how unattractive and wretched you are and crawl in a hole!" Why not switch to interpretations more likely to be so—in other words, try telling yourself the *truth!*

The truth lies in a totally different interpretation of those experiences you have been taking as rejection. Reinterpret those events. Instead of your old, one-track notion that rejection would be so terrible you couldn't stand it because it would mean you are no good, you must begin telling yourself that rejection need not be avoided, that it will certainly occur if you start making overtures to others, and that when it occurs it may mean many things besides documentation of your undesirability.

You don't have to enjoy rejection; nobody does. But you must get your notions about rejection into proportion. It's not the penultimate tragedy you have always assumed. You are not that helpless child you once were, having no way to cope with the thoughtlessness of others. Rather, you now have a grown-up (or growing-up) mind, permeated with the Spirit of Truth to help you look at things in a brand-new and freeing light.

Friend-making involves overriding your long habit of staying in a corner to honor your anxiety, telling yourself the truth and taking action designed to change the quality and number of your relationships.

In the next chapter we will study some practical steps to take to make friends.

FIVE

The Way Out of Loneliness

What would a survey of your social life show? Which of the following would you check?

- ☐ I'm lonely much of the time.
- ☐ I don't have enough friends.
- ☐ I'd like to call someone, but I don't know anybody to call.
- ☐ I have friends, but no one who is really close.
- ☐ No one seems to care what happens to me.
- ☐ There are times when I wish I had more friends.

The statements you found true for you might furnish a starting point. The venture: to discover where changes need to occur. Loneliness could be your word for describing any of the situations on the list.

A RELATIONSHIP JOURNAL

Is it God's time for you to begin working to change your relationship life? Is the overcoming of some form of loneliness one of the objectives? The first step that I recommend is to start keeping a relationship journal. A journal often makes it possible to bring about life changes when no amount of sheer effort or willpower has worked.

If you have never kept a journal and do not know how to begin, buy yourself a small spiral-bound notebook and label it *Relationship Journal.* Your journal will serve as a tool for untwisting the relationships of your life. In this chapter, we will begin working on undoing the snarls of loneliness. Later you will use your journal to chart your progress and to journal your misbeliefs. But for the first step, create a chart of your present relationships.

Here is a sample form suggested by therapist Jeffrey Young. I have created imaginary friends and scores to illustrate.

Current Relationship Rating Chart

	Names				
	Fred	John	Irma	Mary	Jesus
Frequency rating (0–10)	4	8	9	6	5
Disclosure rating (0–10)	1	3	4	3	4
"Caring" rating (0–10)	2	4	8	1	10
Date relationship began	5/81	12/80	6/80	9/82	5/72
Date relationship ended or weakened	10/81				
Reason for ending or weakening	(Fred moved)				

Frequency = the amount of time you and friend spend together

Disclosure = extent able to discuss private thoughts and feelings: the more private, the higher the rating

Caring = how much each friend can be counted on, trusted, depended on, especially in times of crisis

You will notice that the last column is devoted to evaluating your friendship with Jesus. Before you complete this column, read John 15:12–17. Here Jesus describes His relationship with His disciples as a friendship! You began a friendship with Him by being born again, when you were baptized, or when you became a believer. This is the most important of all your friendships, since you have an absolute guarantee of its total goodness—an impossibility in any purely human relationship, however lovely. Ideally, the scores in the *Jesus* column should all be *tens.* But score honestly here—don't write what *should be* but what *is* the case.

Studying your personal chart can help you determine where change is needed. Here is how it works: The sample chart reveals pretty regular meetings with most friends (frequency ratings). All the relationships, however, lack depth and closeness (disclosure ratings).

The sample chart is that of a person who needs to work on revealing himself to others, and engaging in intimate, personal communication. Your chart may reveal very few encounters with others, or even that you have very few friends. Your work at the beginning, then, will be to practice *initiating* and *maintaining* new relationships. In other words, you want to lengthen the list of names and raise the frequency ratings on your chart. If your own *disclosure* rating is low, you will need to risk opening up to others.

The sample chart shows that the person's relationship with Jesus needs attention. Much more time is spent with human friends than in fellowship with the Lord. Furthermore, the relationship with Jesus is not close or intimate. It may be that prayers and Scripture readings are brief and purely formal with no pouring-out of the heart to God. Practice in self-disclosure begins in one's prayer-life: Open up and tell your heavenly Friend your deepest secrets. Your own chart will serve as an indicator of what needs work in your *most significant relationship*.

In general, notice that if you have low ratings for frequency on your chart and/or very few names, you need to give attention to learning how to *initiate* relationships. If you have low disclosure and caring ratings, you need to pay most attention to acquiring the skills for *closer* relationships.

INITIATING MORE FRIENDSHIPS

Let's say that your loneliness results from having very few friends with whom you hardly ever get together.

In such a predicament, you make a big, easy, vulnerable target for the Enemy. His arrows will aim at your mind, and you will propagandize yourself under demonic coaching pretty much as follows:

> *Nobody pursues me, so I know nobody wants me. I must be dull, unattractive, boring, and ugly. Something must be terribly wrong with me, so there's no point in trying to win friends; I'd just get hurt. I can't stand that, so I will go on forever being miserable and lonely. I have no choice.*

As long as you believe such prevarications, you'll make yourself a loser, frozen in isolation, closed to opportunities, and wide open to loneliness and depression. Another part of the usual package: You're not very active; you sit around a lot doing nothing or mindlessly watching low-IQ TV shows. And what have you done for yourself? You've kept yourself safe from rejection. Is it worth it?

REVERSING YOUR DIRECTION

Think back to when you formed your current erroneous beliefs about rejection and your own social stimulus value. You were working within the severe limitations of your little child's mind, very likely, with nothing but the evidence and logic available from your tiny shred of experienced living. You fabricated some of your theories to explain pain generated in certain primary relationships. These facts alone ought to convince you that some of what you've taken for granted is nonsense.

Think on the fact that the love of God, from which all true worth must be derived, assigns you infinite value, eternal significance, and deep interest. Wouldn't you do well to line your own beliefs up with the universe's own *Bureau of Standards*? And doesn't it stand to reason that, if you become active, doing things that have importance to God and interest you instead of vegetating away your spare time, you will be even less likely to seem dull and uninteresting to others?

Reverse not only what goes on in your mind but what you *do* as well. Rather than assuming that people will reach out to you if you are only interesting enough, you will need to initiate and reach out to others. Most people are waiting for someone to show interest in them. If you do, they will respond and will become interested in you.

HANDLING REJECTION

What if someone rejects you? What if it happens more than once? First of all, be sure it's genuine rejection. How do you *know*? Couldn't you be upsetting yourself by misinterpreting the whole thing through the lenses of your radical misbeliefs? No? This time you're really getting the message that the other person doesn't want you now or later. Then here's an opportunity to educate yourself. Pay close attention to how it feels. Is it horrible? Awful? Unendurable? It's painful, sure, just as any other disappointment is painful. But you can stand it, survive it, and come up telling yourself the truth in place of radical misbeliefs.

Notice not only how the rejection feels, but pay attention to the truth about its meaning. Be clear in the head about its significance. It *doesn't* mean you're worthless, that *nobody* will ever want you, that you're a social slug; only that you and this one person appear to be incompatible at the moment; only that here and now, today, that other person believes he or she doesn't need you.

So you need to learn to handle rejection. Here's your chance.

ONE KEY: GET MOVING AGAIN!

Most chronically lonely people have allowed themselves to become inert. Have you dropped your interests? Hobbies? Stopped going out? Let yourself develop all the fascinating attributes of a vegetable?

Kent, the young man I introduced in the previous chapter, had to work through some very typical misbeliefs and attitudes. When we began to work on getting his life out of "park," we came to some of the usual roadblocks.

"I don't feel like doing anything," Kent complained. "I just sit and stare at the TV screen—or gawk at the wall. Nothing is fun anymore. I can't get up any enthusiasm for anything."

I asked, "What are some of the things you used to like doing, Kent?"

"Nothing interests me now. I used to enjoy sports—a lot. And I played guitar in school—some of us guys had a little group. We even wrote our own songs. But I haven't done anything like that for years. I don't even know anybody to do things with."

Maybe you, too, have sunk into paralysis. You spend your evenings glued to the tube, your days off fussing with trivia, or working. You've told yourself until you believe it that nothing would be fun, and things you used to find interesting are now a drag.

Perhaps you even suffer from depression. Many lonely people do. In fact, it's the prevailing mood among the lonely. This misbelief may be yours:

> *I wouldn't enjoy it anyway, so there is no point in doing anything I can avoid.*

Although lonely people are frequently depressed and therefore convinced of this and similar notions leading to inactivity, nothing could be further from the truth. They can and sometimes do discover that the very moment they shake themselves out of their torpor to do things they formerly enjoyed, some of the old enjoyment returns. No matter how negative you feel about resuming once-enjoyable activities, the likelihood is great that *once you get going you will find them interesting again.* Even if it takes a while to become absorbed in such pursuits, you must force yourself to do them, telling yourself the truth that they interested you once and they *will* interest you again.

Why is it so important for lonely people to stoke their interests and start moving again? Because you want success with other people. To get it, you need to be able to sustain momentum in solitary pursuits. You can increase your social stimulus value by submerging yourself in activities and interests that light up your board!

Kent, for example, decided to begin a systematic Bible study program offered by a local Christian fellowship. He developed an intense interest in learning what God has to say to people like himself. He also started running and lifting weights at a fitness center. At first, Kent's sole purpose was to drop forty pounds. But after a few weeks he found pumping iron challenging and began enjoying action for action's sake—it was exhilerating to use his muscles for a change. He began practicing his music, attending some concerts and learning that he could truly enjoy these things by himself.

If you can't stand doing things alone, you may be overdependent on relationships with others to keep you going. Do not skip this step. If you are presently inactive, it is important to begin by activating yourself.

Once you clear away some old misbeliefs, you'll find there's no better preparation for an interesting social life than an interesting life. People who have convinced themselves that they cannot enjoy anything alone and must not even try will discover that it's easier than they thought.

HOW TO GET MOVING AGAIN

Here is a step-by-step method to get yourself moving again. If you are presently apathetic and depressed but willing to work at overcoming loneliness, take these steps one at a time.

First, take a page of your journal and make a list of activities you once found interesting. Include especially activities requiring energetic physical movement: swimming, running, bike riding, fast walking, sports—robust activity is vital. List pursuits that get you out of the house and in contact with other people.

Think first of activities likely to bring you into dialogue with the very Word of God, because that Word is the source of the abundant life Jesus came to give us. Think also of church activities that will involve you in the company of fellow Christians. Later, when you come to the point of initiating friendships, you will want to make your closest and deepest relationships with others who share your most significant commitment.

Second, select activities from your list and construct a schedule for your free time during the coming week. If you can think of an old friend you could call and invite to do something, include this. Leave time to be quiet before God and time for healthful rest, but no time for vegetating.

Third, carry out your plans. Follow the schedule you have made as closely as possible. *Even if you don't feel like doing anything.*

Fourth, keep a record in your journal. Alongside your recorded activities, write out, *as it occurs to you*, your problem-centered self-talk. Discover the misbeliefs in your self-talk and underscore them. You will probably find they come thick and fast as you think about engaging in play or hobbies, or as you look forward to calling your friend. Get them all down. Then vigorously attack the untruth in your misbeliefs, energetically replacing the falsehoods with the truth.

Fifth, when you have gotten moving again, and are nicely immersed in interests and activities, it's time to initiate a new relationship. Call someone you have met but have not yet done anything with. Arrange to do something together. In case you can think of absolutely no one, you will need to attend groups or classes where you can make contacts with new people, especially with people who share your faith in Jesus Christ. Keep initiating relationships with people who interest you. This step is to become habitual. Go through life initiating—moving out toward others. Don't let anything persuade you to go back into your shell. Even if at first you n't very pleased with your successes, keep at it. You'll have *some* winners, despite the risks you're taking.

REPLACING RADICAL LONELINESS MISBELIEFS WITH THE TRUTH

Meanwhile, continue your journal. Observe your self-talk as you plan and initiate new contacts and record the misbeliefs you find there. Ask God to reveal the *radex*, or root notions, you formed in the context of primary relationships. Ask Him to show you by His work of *revealing* the childhood contexts and events that gave impetus to your early theorizing. Keep careful notes in your journal, recording your memories and other discoveries. Clearly spell out the misbeliefs, past and present, that are keeping you lonely. They will need to be met and challenged with the truth if you are going to change your social behavior.

Doubtless, you will find in your own head some of the rejection misbeliefs we've already discussed. As you reach the point of assertively letting someone know you want to get acquainted, you'll tell yourself all sorts of foolishness. These notions generate fear; you become so fearful of the other person's reaction that you won't let yourself approach anybody. If you swallow these misbeliefs whole, they'll take you back to where you started—in social never-never land!

MISBELIEFS TO KEEP YOU LONELY

Here they are—the ideas designed to keep you in your shell.

I'm not worth loving. I am unlikable. I'm bad. Something I can't discern is wrong with me.

I'm no good at communicating, so I can't make friends. I don't go anywhere, I'm not interested in anything, I'm not good at any sports, I'm not up on the latest political news, I never read anything, I can't ever think of anything to talk about—so I can't possibly make friends.

I don't let my feelings show, so I can't ever have close relationships.

My marriage failed, proving something's wrong with me. I must be incapable of a good relationship with anyone.

Relationships that don't last forever are no good. It's better not to get involved because the relationship will end and I'll be hurt (again). None of my relationships last, so they're failures.

The other person should be as strongly committed as I am or I can't have a relationship. Unless he gives precisely the same as I do, the friendship is no good. The other person has to care as much as I do or I can't help being miserable.

I'm boring, dull, and uninteresting, so no one will want to spend much time with me.

I can't think of anything to talk about, so no one will like being with me.

THE TRUTH ABOUT RELATIONSHIPS

With such notions rattling around in your head, the Enemy can then step in and fulfill his design: to keep you under his control so that you remain isolated from others and grow more and more wretched and lonely.

The truth is that nothing God created is intrinsically bad. Remember that God declared every item in His creation "very good" (Gen. 1:31). I believe God looked forward as well as backward, surveying future history and generations yet unborn. In that all-encompassing glance over the entire creation—past, present, and future—God saw *you* and declared what He had made very good. Marred, as the rest of the human race is, by sin, yet intrinsically *very good*. As a matter of fact, your misbeliefs to the contrary, *no one is just plain intrinsically unlovable*.

If you have difficulty with communication or with showing your feelings, you can learn how to do those things. If you really can't think of anything to talk about, you can show interest in what the other person has to say.

If you have let yourself go and your appearance is sloppy and unattractive, you can spend some time and resources on cleanliness, neatness and attractive dress that is appropriate.

If you have made errors in past relationships, those errors don't prove you have some fatal inborn defect. Instead, they point the way to new learning—to new directions for changing your behavior.

The truth is that participants in a relationship are rarely committed and caring at a precisely equal level at any given time. *Feelings, level of investment* and *caring* fluctuate. The partner who is giving the most at one time may be receiving the most at another time. In any case, it isn't necessary to be miserable if you care more than someone else in a relationship. It won't hurt you to give more than you get. You have the word of the Lord Jesus on it. (See Acts 20:35.)

Finally, relationships are not awful just because they come to an end. All human affairs are transient. Nothing lasts forever on this earth. Very few friendships or even love relationships last for a lifetime, and even if they do they must eventually end with the death of one or the other person. It is nonsense to insist that a relationship that cannot be guaranteed to last forever isn't worth forming.

"BUT COULDN'T I BE PUTTING PEOPLE OFF?"

Sometimes our behavior does put people off. Occasionally, the problem can amount to poor social behavior, lack of cleanliness or slovenly personal grooming. This book cannot deal with such issues, but they are important. Don't overlook them. If you have problems like these, develop new habits. New social skills could revolutionize your life.

Very frequently, people who have been fearfully avoiding

others don't know exactly how to go about initiating and deepening relationships. Then loneliness is not due to misbeliefs alone, but also to lack of practice in the necessary social skills.

Here are some of the indicators suggesting that social skills training might be part of the solution to a person's social difficulties:

- You can't think of anything to say; you are often speechless; the other person must do all or almost all of the talking. Others say you are distant, hard to get to know.
- You feel nervous, flustered, tense, anxious when you are conversing with someone else. You are so distracted by your anxiety and tension that you can't listen attentively to the other person.
- You are passive. Others take advantage of you. You don't know how to say no, or to ask for what you want. You find yourself feeling resentful about the way others treat you, but you don't know how to handle the situation.
- You talk most of the time, making it difficult for the other person to say anything. If he does manage to say something, you ignore it or barely acknowledge it. You interrupt. You talk loudly about yourself or your affairs regardless of whether anyone is interested. You boast, brag and exalt yourself. You try so hard to impress others that you end by alienating them.
- You run yourself down constantly, practically begging other people to tell you that you are wonderful.
- You open up to others much too soon, before the relationship is ready for it. You tell others your intimate secrets, deficits and faults before the other person has even begun to tell you anything about himself.
- You put others down, complain, use sarcasm, predict negative outcomes and criticize a good deal so that most of your speech is unpleasant to hear.
- You don't look others in the eye, face the person you're

talking to, wear appropriate facial expressions, or appear to be paying attention to the other person.

If you suspect that you have any of these characteristics, you would do well to seek the services of a helping person. It is my opinion that you probably can't resolve difficulties of this kind by reading a book. You need to work with another person who is knowledgeable and experienced in social skills training. If, after studying this list carefully, you believe that this is where the problem lies, find a Christian therapist with the requisite training and experience to teach you appropriate social behavior.

GOING DEEPER

Jesus developed different kinds of relationships with different people. In this, as in everything, He set an example for us. He ministered to multitudes, but they didn't all become His followers or His friends. Yet He did have a wide circle of friends of both sexes. Within that circle He enjoyed more intimacy with Peter, James and John. Finally, He had one particularly intimate friend who leaned affectionately on His breast at the last supper. This was John, "the disciple whom Jesus loved."

Most people need at least one close friendship. Some will enjoy several. Nonetheless, relationships on this level of intimacy are not common. They offer more than ordinary friendships. In a very close relationship, two people approach 100 percent openness with each other, revealing their deepest selves, and sharing their most profound thoughts, commitments and feelings.

Let's say that you have begun doing the things you've read about so far. You've made a start, forming relationships with several people with whom you've done some things. Now you would like to deepen some of your new friendships, to taste and enjoy intimacy with others. So it's appropriate to move forward with one or two of your casual friends. Maybe you have never had any trouble forming casual friendships, but haven't known how to move beyond the superficial acquaintance level. By learning to open up to others, we can develop friendships that go beyond the superficial and offer the satisfaction of deeper levels of closeness and intimacy.

We will probably find that most of our relationships do not involve massive amounts of self-disclosure and cannot really be considered *close* friendships. There is nothing wrong with that. Some of our relationships, perhaps a dozen or so, will be more intimate and open, but in these we remain somewhat less than totally open about all that is within us. With these friends, we will reveal more of ourselves than we do to those on the first level, and they will do the same with us. With a few of our friends we will want to develop greater openness and trust. With them, we will exchange more personal information. Finally, with one or two very special friends, we will open our inmost selves as much as possible, sharing thoughts and feelings we find difficult to tell to anyone.

HOW TO BEGIN GETTING CLOSE

Start gradually. It is a mistake to dump your entire mental and emotional storage bin on someone with whom you are trying to deepen a relationship. Jesus began to reveal His innermost thoughts about His purpose and His aims only after He and His disciples had been companions for some time. (See Matthew 16.)

You might begin by telling your new friend about a personal problem you're working on. Or describe a feeling you would like to share with someone else. Then encourage your friend to do the same, perhaps by asking appropriate questions: "Do *you* ever feel that way?" or "Have *you* ever experienced anything like that?"

As you move toward greater closeness with another person, tell your friend about such inner "secrets" as your notions of inferiority or your fears of becoming dependent on the other. Misgivings, irritations, positive feelings toward the other person, appreciation—all these and other thoughts are grist for the intimacy mill. And remember to let the other person share reciprocally with you. Listen, don't just talk.

One important caution: When your friend begins to share intimate thoughts or feelings with you, resist any temptation you may have to "straighten things out" by rebuking or lecturing. If you clobber someone for sharing what he has feared to tell anyone else, you will only convince him that the fear was justified and that he shouldn't have told you either. No intimacy can grow out of that. Tell yourself the truth: God has called you to be a friend, not to shape this person up to your specifications.

As some of these relationships ripen and develop, they will move increasingly toward 100 percent openness. Do you have a better definition for a close relationship? I believe total openness between two people is what a close relationship means. This was the quality of the relationship between Jesus and His friend, John. The other disciples knew that John had access to Jesus' innermost thoughts, meanings and intentions. (See John 13:21ff.)

HOW TO DEAL WITH ANTI-INTIMACY MISBELIEFS

Perhaps you have never thought about intimacy with others as something you could attain. Just as you assumed new friendships happen all by themselves, you imagined that closeness, whenever it popped into your life, would just happen—that it would generate itself.

Closeness never comes by spontaneous generation. When you consider drawing close to another, misbeliefs will pound your mind. "You can't do that because. . . ." Might such thoughts even now be insinuating themselves into your internal monologue?

Because developing intimacy involves doing what seems frightening, making close friendships requires trying things you aren't accustomed to. Meanwhile, you must combat the thoughts and beliefs that have so long supported your lonely isolation. The misbeliefs will come along to put the brakes on your changing. Be prepared to tolerate some anxiety without using it as an excuse to back out or stop trying. The moment difficulty arises in a relationship, you may experience a panicky, frustrated, or angry impulse to get out before the other person does. You may want to throw it all away just to get even. So every maturing friendship sooner or later runs into obstacles. Here is a list of the most common. The other person

- forgets a commitment;
- cancels an engagement you were looking forward to;
- forgets something important to you;
- fails to notice what you did out of the goodness of your heart;
- seems to take you for granted;
- doesn't return your phone call;
- criticizes you;
- appears bored;
- values another friend more than you;
- repeatedly seeks his own way;
- disparages your favorite activity;
- neglects showing you attention;
- behaves discourteously;
- lets you see negative moods you haven't noticed before;
- takes no initiative, while you've initiated several times;
- waits for you to call *all* the time.

That's far from a complete list, for relationship problems are many and troublesome. What I want to emphasize here is that, especially for lonely people, any of these events or others like them can prompt an unwarranted exit from a friendship. Don't let any of this ruin your relationships. And don't think something has gone terribly wrong when you encounter such obstacles. You *will*!

MISBELIEFS AND THE IMPULSE TO ESCAPE

Have you talked to yourself this way?

What kind of friendship is this? He doesn't care about me, and he doesn't think about me as much as I think about him. He hasn't even acknowledged the gift I sent. Maybe I ought to be cool, act like I don't care either. Don't call, don't write, don't be so cordial if he calls. I'll show him!

Does any of that have a familiar ring to it?
What about this?

She says she can't go to the concert with me again! It's tiresome to be turned down so often. She expects me to go with her when it's her idea. Obviously, she can't handle a friendship she can't control. I don't want a friend like that! I'd better get out while I feel mad enough to stay away!

If you experience the urge to end a friendship or to hurt the other person just a bit to pay him back for acting contrary to your "perfectly reasonable" expectations, it's time to capture your own untruthful self-talk and change yourself.

Take your journal in hand and carefully record your thoughts. You will discover misbeliefs among them, and many will sound like the following. These misbeliefs will appear true, so don't let yourself be seduced by the Enemy into accepting them uncritically and terminating your friendship.

My friend doesn't like me anymore. And what did I expect? I always lose everybody I like. This is just another failure. Might as well give up. I couldn't even make my mother and father love me. I'd better get out of this one before I really get hurt.

I'm not as interesting to her as she is to me. Obviously, I care more than she does. I can't tolerate a relationship like that. So forget her.

Others should pursue me. If they really like me, they will. If I have to keep pursuing them, it means they don't find me interesting or attractive.

Maybe if I stay away, he will feel bad, and apologize.

He thinks I'm not very important and that he can get away with slighting me. But I do have my pride! I can't let him get away with it.

I can't stand her liking someone else more than me. Of course, she likes me, too, but not as much. I have to be first, or not at all!

It's outrageous that I have to do most of the asking. Things should be even. If they're not even, I want out.

It's wretched that my friend hasn't noticed how much I've sacrificed for the friendship. I need friends who are sensitive and caring.

This whole project is discouraging! It proves again that I'm no good at making friends or getting close. I learned, when I was a child, that something is wrong with me.

Please notice these *truths*:

It is not necessary or effective to run away the moment such troubles arise. Remember, you don't have to play it safe.

Although behaviors like those listed may annoy and discomfit you, they are not the disasters you may believe them to be.

Such difficulties as I have listed are not unusual. On the contrary, some of them will occur in the course of most developing friendships. They are quite common.

You must learn to stop interpreting events like these as catastrophic and doom-laden and begin taking them in stride as opportunities to learn new skills and new self-control options.

Very likely, the other person does not see things as

you do. Your friend would be very surprised to hear your view of the matter.

Even if your friend is guilty of a thoughtless breach of courtesy or an unintentional slight to you, it's no catastrophe. You can survive and so can your relationship. If it's something that occurs repeatedly and it's very significant to you, talk to your friend about it. If not, talk to yourself about it and tell yourself the truth.

It is perfectly all right to keep on initiating, to call the other person more than he calls you and to give more than you receive in a relationship. You don't have to keep tallying up the score to see if things are even. And you will be happier if you refuse to keep track.

Just because you would react to your friend in a particular way does not mean you should expect him to react to you in the same way. Your behavior is not a norm or standard for others to follow.

There is no reason why other people should fulfill your expectations, even if they are, in your view, perfectly reasonable.

You must stop interpreting today's relationships through the lenses of your radical misbeliefs, acquired when you were too little to discern the truth about relationships!

Thoughtful readers will already see that these truths merely apply Christian love to relationships between friends. John wrote that "perfect love casts out fear" (1 John 4:18).

Lonely people suffer from fear. They honor their anxiety. Instead of moving out to find and love others, *even though this means tolerating some anxiety,* they move away from others so they don't feel anxious about rejection or slights. By opting for temporary comfort instead of putting up with risk and anxiety, they keep themselves hurting from the infinitely greater pain of loneliness. If you are lonely, you may decide to continue avoiding initiative in relationships.

If you do, you will give anxiety the power to disrupt your life. You will continue honoring your anxiety as if it were a little god, and anxiety will dominate you.

But if you will tell yourself the truth, combat your radical relationship misbeliefs and your other relationship misbeliefs with truth, and initiate and work at relationships in love, you will be able to see how the application of God's perfect love can and will cast out fear.

SIX

Childhood Trauma and the "Right-Person" Misbelief

Many relationships come to a needless end because of the operation of this falsehood:

There is someone somewhere who will fulfill me.

Do you believe there is a *right person*? Do you console yourself with the notion that that right person will come along and make your dreams come true? Do you tell yourself:

My right person will surely meet all my needs. The pain and emptiness, the frustration, the failure to have true meaning, my desperate need for love—when finally I find the right person, all will be fulfilled. Or, now that I've found my right person, I'm entitled to have all my dreams come true!

The right person—what a charming notion! Its seductive emanations weave their way through romance in books and films. It hits you over the head in fairy tales. ("Someday, my prince will come, someday I'll find my love, and how thrilling that moment will be.")

Plato wrote about it in the *Symposium,* suggesting that in some primordial age, a troublemaker among the gods chopped mortals in two, with the permanent result that we are born as incomplete halves. Each must seek until he finds his other half, the one person who, being joined to him in relationship, will fit like the other side of a torn dollar bill.

Some ancient Bible teachers speculated similarly, conjecturing that in the creation of Eve (Gen. 2), God split an originally androgynous Adam down the middle, separating the first human being into a male half and a female half. So each of us must wander the world until he locates and joins his proper "other half."

One day a man asked me to review his situation and tell him if he was married to the "wrong person." His request implied that there was a "right person" for him somewhere.

Most of us have at one time or another told ourselves we would marry that one right person. Or we have waited a lifetime for a friend whose mental and emotional and personality "shape" would conform perfectly to our own—the perfect match. Is it your belief that there is a right person somewhere waiting for you to form a friendship, a romance, a marriage?

Even after you have a good friend or a marriage you thought would be perfect, do you ask yourself dubiously whether the friend or spouse you have is that perfect match which, you believe, must exist somewhere just for you? Are you puzzled and grieved because the person of your dreams hasn't met all your needs and truly fulfilled you as you expected?

CHARLOTTE'S STORY

The right-person theme originates in the context of primary relationships. That's how it came about for Charlotte. But as you will see, nobody sat her down and lectured right person concepts into her head. It's more complex and subtle than that. Bear in mind that Charlotte's story is her own. No two persons have the same history, and though they may carry similar radical misbeliefs through life, each will have a different account to give of its origin. The origin of Charlotte's misbelief was horrifying.

Agonizing memories returned vividly to mind as she worked in counseling back to a time before she was even ten years old. Pushing through waves of pain to recover the history she had closed off to control the anguish, she had to face the fact that she would never understand her father's sadism. Why had he always sought *her* out when anything upset him? If the car wouldn't start, if the neighbor's dog ruined his shrubs, if the darkness shaded his eyes when he came home from work in the late afternoon, Charlotte trembled at what lay ahead for her. She would wait in her bedroom for the storm she knew would savage her.

Sometimes the sound of his boots clumping up the stairs wrenched her out of sleep. Her fear escalated to panic as he kicked open the door to her tiny room. Never did he utter a word of explanation, never a warning. Grim, tense, silent, this man-turned-beast would tear the child from her warm bed and beat her until his rage spent itself. Occasionally he followed the beatings with a worse horror; he would caress his small daughter's genitals and force her to have intercourse.

Since her father never spoke of them either during or after these episodes, since Charlotte's mother resolutely denied the problem, and since no one else ever knew, the hapless child was left with no explanation. Because she had to know why, like all children, she did what all children do. Lacking an answer, she invented one. She constructed her own hypothesis to explain what was turning her life into ongoing horror.

Charlotte reasoned that she was bad. She felt dirty to the core, so she must be very bad. Otherwise, why would her father punish her so severely? To her child's mind, it was unthinkable that her father could be bad; he was an adult and adults were good. They were always right. That meant Charlotte was wrong—wrong and bad. She hated herself for being so awful, and she loathed herself most in the aftermath of her father's attacks. And then, as she grew, something else triggered in the recesses of her mind.

God equipped the mind with wondrous devices for its own protection. Why didn't this girl reduce into gibbering insanity? How did she keep her reason? When there is no other way to peace, we all possess the capacity to deliberately forget. There is a price that must be paid later, but forgetting can help a child through the immediate crisis. Charlotte did her best to forget. And in putting the terrible memories out of her consciousness, she made use of another gift of the Creator—the gift of imagination. Forgetting the real world, Charlotte made room for an alternative world, a world fashioned of wishes, hopes and dreams.

By the time she was eleven, Charlotte had created her own version of the right-person misbelief. Huddled alone in her secret refuge, a woodland glade near her home, she constructed a hypothesis to make sense and furnish meaning amid the horrors of her everyday existence. Meanwhile, she did her best to obliterate every painful recollection of her father's lustful brutality. She taught herself to live by dreaming, and out of her dreams she drew material for fashioning her hypothesis, her radical misbelief. She used it as a bandage to cover the wounds in her soul.

She dreamed of having a father who truly loved her. She made herself feel his strong arms holding her, created pictures of his parental devotion poured out on her little person. This perfect father fulfilled all her wants, loved her unconditionally, without any demands, and made her feel she was lovable and good instead of polluted and bad. These dreams became more than wishes. The imaginings became beliefs. Someday she would find that person whose unconditional love would meet all her needs and fulfill all her aspirations. That person would ask nothing whatever of Charlotte. And such love would make her believe she was not bad, but good.

Charlotte had now formulated her right-person radical misbelief. She clung tightly to it until she gained courage to face the truth and tell it to herself.

CREATING YOUR OWN RIGHT-PERSON RADICAL MISBELIEF

Many people, like Charlotte, first formulate their right-person dreams as an upbeat fantasy in counterpoint to a humiliating and degrading childhood relationship. A parent's violent mistreatment; a traumatic nightmare of persecution by peers; sexual abuse and degradation by an older relative; even unremitting, wilting tongue-lashing over months and years can pose a seemingly insoluble problem.

Fantasy comes to the rescue and the little one creates imaginary balm to spread on smarting mental wounds. It is as if she is telling herself, "None of my wishes makes any difference to anyone now, so I must be very bad. But someday, someone will love me without limit and such love will make everything perfect. Then I will be able to believe I am good."

Because such lives as Charlotte's are hidden from our eyes, most of us give little thought to the suffering with which multitudes of children must pass their growing years, targets of unrestrained cruelty or lust. Even those who had experiences like Charlotte's have, in many cases, pushed their days of misery to a forgotten mental corner.

These childhood nightmares are far more common than many imagine.[1] And some who have endured similar scenes have so totally repressed them that they are unaware of their own past anguish. Some may recall childhood dread and terror similar to Charlotte's experiences, while some

---

[1]Numbers telling the complete truth are impossible to obtain. For example, statistics on physical abuse of children include only cases where visible physical wounds are inflicted—broken bones, bruises and lacerations apparent on physical examination. Charlotte and many others would never be counted in such statistics. Estimates are available. Many more children than come to the attention of physicians suffer physical abuse. The United States Government Department of Health and Human Services published statistics on sexual abuse in 1985. According to these estimates, one in every four or five girls and one in every nine or ten boys are sexually abused before they reach age eighteen.

may remember more subtle, indirect abuse. Some will have so forcefully expelled their experiences from awareness that they can recall them only with extreme effort, perhaps a special work of *revealing* by the Spirit of God. It even happens, at times, that parents who do all things well are nevertheless perceived as abusive by a child who has unwittingly misinterpreted their meanings and intentions. In such cases, God desires to work a *revealing* of the less-malignant factual state of affairs, for such distortions occur through destructive demonic interference in family relationships.

Other histories out of which the right-person radical misbelief may grow involve the child's perception of rejection by parents or friends. Some form of relationship difficulty, at any rate, ordinarily furnishes the soil out of which this root notion springs. Sometimes, an adult model who holds to and reveals his own right-person radical misbelief may be simply copied by a growing child who grows up with the same unrealistic expectations as his model.

SEARCHING FOR THE RIGHT PERSON

When Charlotte grew up, she set out to find her very own right person. She thought this person would satisfy her old hunger for the love of a tender, caring father. He would devote himself to her unstintingly, asking nothing from her in return. And she could stop believing she was bad. Charlotte had no parental models from whom to experience the reality of human love. Her notion of love was an invention, made of her needs, wishes and dreams. For this woman, *love* was a fairytale word. A magic formula.

What Charlotte believed was unreal: She felt that when she at last found a man who lived up to her invented image of love, he would only want to fulfill her. With no needs of his own, this godlike creature would give her unlimited love. Never once did it enter Charlotte's mind that one who loved her rightly might expect some return from her.

Yet inner conflicts persisted. Charlotte began seeing a middle-aged, self-styled counselor who worked with people in his home. He talked a good deal about "selfless Christian love," a concept Charlotte used to buttress her own belief about the love to which she was entitled. She began to see her counselor as one who truly loved in the manner he described. Before long, the two of them were having extended talks for the purpose of helping her. Occasionally, the counselor showed his "love" by holding Charlotte close "to comfort her when she felt bad." It was just as she'd pictured the selfless, warm love of an ideal father who was kind, understanding and giving. Charlotte thought her deepest longings were now fulfilled. She was pleased that her right-person expectations had been so wondrously fulfilled.

Soon the counselor held her for most of their session. One day he touched her genitals. She felt embarrassed, wrong. "But still," Charlotte told herself, "it's not a big thing. And if it pleases him, it's not much to ask, considering all he's giving me. I suppose it's all right."

Before long, the man told Charlotte she needed more intense experiences of love. He suggested she go to bed with him. She was afraid: afraid to refuse, and afraid she might lose her fulfiller. She gave in. Afterwards, Charlotte felt terrible. Guilt and remorse flooded her. She blamed herself for being such a bad person. It had to be her fault. What was there about her that always made this bad thing happen? It was the same miserable filthiness she had felt following her own father's assaults. There must be something very evil about her. She knew it now, for sure. And she would have to end her friendship with the counselor. Depressed, hating herself, blaming only her own wickedness, Charlotte found herself alone. In this desperate state, she felt that the right person had to come along to rescue her.

She went out with men, usually with men a little older than herself. But most of them talked endlessly about themselves and seemed interested only in their own affairs. They always wanted something from her—usually it was sex.

At last, Charlotte met her Prince Charming—a man who wanted nothing so much as a wife and children. For a time she was certain that Paul was the one. Now her dreams really would come true. Now she had found her right person for sure. Paul would fulfill her. He would be the selfless, all-giving one. She married him with these high hopes. But it soon became clear that Paul expected his wife to have sex with him more often than she would have preferred. He also turned out to have an interest in sports and wanted some time to pursue it. She had not counted on those things. She had never imagined he would put her aside to pursue his own wishes. Her fantasies had never made room for a real person with feelings, wants and needs. By the time their little boy was born, Charlotte had come to realize with dismay that Paul would never fill the space her dreams had carved out for him.

Now her depression became severe. Charlotte came for treatment. We want to tell you enough about Charlotte's treatment to show you how misbeliefs come to light. Charlotte discussed her relationship with Paul: She insisted he didn't love her, that she couldn't feel any love from him. Then she discovered an entrenched conviction that no one loved her. We puzzled over that, because she had many friends. Finally, exploring Charlotte's primary relationships, the story of her father came to light. At last we understood! Of course no one loved her—not in the sense of her fantasies, her unrealistic beliefs about love! Because she had never had love as a child, this young woman had been forced to invent her own definition of the word out of her dreams. As a result, she had cooked up a phenomenon so unreal it did not exist in a human being—yet she had spent her life looking for it.

There could be no *right person*. Charlotte would have to find the love of God. Only His absolute love could feed her hunger. To seek Him in a human being was idolatry.

THE RIGHT-PERSON THEORY IS CORRECT!

As God does His work of *revealing*, we will courageously face the shattering of the *right-person theory* because it is a radical misbelief. Nevertheless, there is a marvelous, grand truth hidden in the right-person belief. In one sense, it is absolutely true. There really is a right person.

God, in His Word, has revealed Jesus as the One right person who can and will fulfill every inchoate or explicit longing of our hearts. "All the promises of God," writes Paul, "find their Yes in him" (2 Cor. 1:20). When you found your faith on Jesus, the right-person theory is no myth. It's absolute truth. Martin Luther sang in triumph, "The right Man [is] on our side, the Man of God's own choosing."

In addition, you may believe God has chosen a person for you—chosen your mate, chosen your friend—and he is therefore a gift from God. In that sense, it is a spiritual fact that certain persons are right for you because God has made you a gift of them.

But we want to focus on the *right-person misbelief.*

THE MISBELIEF

The error is to press this belief beyond its limits. If you are putting all your weight on a human being, believing that person will have to meet your needs and solve your problems, you are believing a lie. Whether that person has already taken a role in your life or has not yet appeared, he will disappoint you, and your relationship will collapse because you've made the creature an idol, a substitute for God's right Man! This radical misbelief makes a creature your god, for a god is anything you fear, love, or trust ultimately.

Here is the pathological version of the right-person misbelief:

> *There is a person somewhere who will meet all my needs and solve all my problems, asking nothing from me in return. When I find him/her, my life will be complete. I'll be happy ever after.*

If this is your radical relationship misbelief, you can probably recognize its seductive promises that keep you looking longingly forward for that future relationship which never comes. But there are other signs of the man or woman who is looking for that right person.

- If you have a streak of the right-person misbelief in you, you go into new relationships with high expectations. You believe for a while you've discovered the right person at long last. You are thrilled because you think that here is your special someone who is going to be perfect for you. Invariably, you are disappointed when you meet reality.

- You have probably been conned, seduced, or taken for a ride in some of your relationships because your misbelief prevents you from taking a good hard look *before* you get involved.

- When you have been used or hurt, you revert to your old theorizing to explain it all: "I must be a bad person." The feeling of being bad hangs around, and you can find ample evidence of your badness, even if you have to invent it!

- When your mate or your friends don't love you unconditionally, you get upset and think the world has tilted on its axis. This violates your expectations, part of your radical misbelief.

- Always seeking, never finding. This is because you believe so strongly in that perfect relationship.

- Someone who loves you balks at the demand that he or she give and give, but never ask anything at all from you.

- Or you are surrounded by people who actually try to give without any return and believe your expectation that they should love you unconditionally. They try, but they don't satisfy you, because no one can until you change your beliefs.

- You expect your mate or your friend to be the perfect parent you never had.

- You are sad, disappointed, frustrated, or depressed a lot, believing you are so bad and that the people who love you aren't worth much either.

- When another relationship disappoints you, you tell yourself, "I've been wrong again. Once again I put all my hopes in someone who seemed so right, only to discover that the person had self-interested motives all along. He did not meet my expectations after all. Another wrong person."

REVEALING, REQUIRING, RESTORING

If any of this sounds somewhat like your own self-talk and history, you will need God's *revealing activity*. And you will be *required* by God to open yourself and your secrets with courageous honesty. The likelihood that you will discover your fundamental problem by yourself without any revelation from God isn't great, because the deception you have participated in for many years is so strong. It is difficult to grasp how greatly you have been mesmerized by this radical misbelief and for how long. It's wrenching to give up this notion, because it has meant everything to you for years. In fact, this notion may have been all that kept you going through repeated disillusionments. The idea of losing your hope of a right person seems to rob your life of its meaning. But this belief must go if you want God's *restoring*.

HOW THE RIGHT-PERSON THEME TWISTS RELATIONSHIPS

One way to recognize your own reliance on the right-person misbelief is to scrutinize the natural history of your relationships.

Are you usually disappointed in them? Are you the one who initiates friendships with high hopes and great expectations, only to find yourself inevitably confronted by the other person's failure to perform as you'd hoped and expected? Do you start with a bang and then find that the other person inevitably disillusions you? Initially you're certain you've found love at last. The new person looks good, wants to know you better and exudes enthusiasm just as you do. You sense the promise of a great friendship, while your mind races with all sorts of plans for the two of you. Then—trouble. You don't understand what could have gone wrong. The other person

fails you;

is late;

stands you up;

doesn't seem as enthusiastic as before;

doesn't call you;

rarely expresses caring anymore;

makes requests or even demands you think unreasonable;

violates what you believe every right-thinking person accepts as "the rules."

Do you discover disparities in all your important relationships between what you expect and what the other person does? For instance:

- You expected your friend to want to spend her day off with you, but she didn't.
- You expected your children to do more to observe your birthday, but they only sent cards and took you out for a dinner.
- You expected your pastor to care so much about you that he would visit you and ask why you haven't been attending church the past three Sundays—but he hasn't said a word, hasn't even called you.
- You expect your guests to offer to help you with the dishes, but they hardly ever do.
- You expect people to do for you at least what you do for them, but they rarely do.
- You expected your parents to volunteer to help you out of your financial morass, but they never said a word about a gift or even a loan—and they can afford it.
- You expect people to give to you the equivalent of what

you give to them and more, but they don't.

- You expect your buddy to be a good listener, but instead he talks about himself a lot.
- You expect your doctor, at least, to infallibly and perfectly attend to your needs rather than have any of his own, but you suspect even he may not be 100 percent committed to you.

MARRIAGE

Marriage is the relationship *par excellence* for claiming right-person expectations. Consider what two right-person believers can do to each other when they get their misbeliefs together in marriage. They expect:

> *Marriage will lift my depression, resolve my anxieties, solve my problems. Though I am unhappy now, marriage is the solution. It will make me happy at last. I'm tired of handling life's burdens and I need someone to take care of me. I'll find that in my marriage.*

The only thing they don't expect is the truth that each of them is getting a partner with expectations as extravagant as his own!

Here are some of the expectations right-person believers may bring into marriage:

He expects: The money I earn is mine. Of course, I'll let her have some to spend for the two of us and our common purposes.

She expects: The money will be *ours*. He will be working for me; and I'll work, too, of course.

He expects: I will consult her on some things, and she'll be so pleased when I let her make some decisions and contribute to others.

She expects: I will decide everything about the household and we'll decide together on big things.

He expects: She'll be so glad I want to save money for retirement so we can be together a lot more.

She expects: He knows we need so much now, so he won't worry about retirement and won't ever think of wanting to stay around home underfoot all the time.

He expects: She'll understand that I want to work overtime, go bowling and spend some time with the guys—they're my old buddies.

She expects: He'll surely want to spend every spare minute with me and the kids—just how he was during our courtship—couldn't get enough time together to suit him.

He expects: We don't have to talk a lot to enjoy each other. We can always watch the stock car races together. She's interested in the same things I am.

She expects: What we'll talk about and communicate deeply about is our problems. There are a few things I want him to change. We want to get close and communicate and I know he'll be so glad to discuss everything openly.

He expects: I'll get all the sex I want, and I won't have to work so hard to seduce her.

She expects: He'll want only to love me and care for me with feelings. Oh yes, our love will include sexual intercourse—sometimes, when I feel like being really nice to him.

He expects: She will take responsibility, pick up my socks and keep my drawer full of clean ones, neatly sorted.

She expects: He will take over the role of my daddy—the perfect one I've always dreamed of.

You may not have to imagine the bitter resentment in store for these pairs of disappointed expectations on two legs—because if you hold *right-person* misbeliefs, you will already have run smack into some bitter disillusionments, whether in marriage or other relationships.

Unfortunately, experience with countless couples has made us aware that most resist the real truth. Namely, that the problem is in their misbeliefs and *not* in the fact that the other person is not a special blend of St. John, Robert Redford, and Santa Claus all rolled into one heroic, heavenly, he-man husband—or, a mysteriously marvelous mixture of Florence Nightingale, Darryl Hannah, Helen of Troy, Grace Kelly, and St. Catherine all packed neatly into one classy, storybook wife. Nor are those bent on meeting their "dream friend" especially eager to revise their misbeliefs rather than chalk up their feelings of letdown to the failures of others.

HOW TO TURN THINGS AROUND

One of the key ingredients in Charlotte's healing was our gentle venture into the past she had fought to prevent reliving, even in thought. Our exploration involved careful, tentative uncovering of the gouges in her soul, carved by her reflections on her traumatic interactions with her father. Until this material became accessible to Charlotte's consciousness, she was victimized by it but unable to cope with the meanings she had derived (erroneously) from it.

It may be that, like this woman, some readers have discovered much about themselves, faced down many current misbeliefs and interjected a measure of truth, so they now enjoy some new freedom. But they still find themselves defeated *especially in relationships*. Again and again they enter friendships with enthusiasm and new resolve, only to find their disappointments make mockery of their great expectations.

They hardly dare hope now, because they are sure that every relationship balloon will pop, every flower wither, every hope turn to disillusionment. They can't tell why. They haven't found the key.

When you hit a wall, it may turn out that exploring the origins of your misbeliefs will furnish the key you need to see clearly by giving you a new perspective. This is why researching the past is sometimes a valid enterprise in emotional healing.

There is no way we can change the past. Nor do we wish to alter our memories, even the bad ones, for such alteration is the stuff of which illness comes. But we do want to find and alter our early false interpretations of events. For likely as not, we operate with their residue today. For Charlotte, it wasn't possible even to notice her right-person misbelief until we retraced the scenes in which it was formulated. For you, too, primary relationships that were disillusioning and disappointing may have been the impetus for creating your own misbeliefs. As you work to turn things around, look to the roots of your own right-person misbeliefs. You may discover there the key to releasing ideas you haven't been able to budge.

WHAT YOU CAN DO TO GET BETTER

If it's beginning to dawn on you that nobody is ever going to come along who will fulfill all your needs and wants, nobody will love you forever without regard to your behavior and nobody will cater to you for a lifetime without a thought for anything else, you're already getting better. If it's beginning to dawn on you that it's not other people and their terrible failures to live up to your standards, but your expectations which are ruining your most precious relationships, you have already come a long way.

It's the dawn of a new day for you when you can look to yourself. You're ready to move ahead then, and the next step is prayer for healing within yourself, because *you* are the repository of most of your relationship twists. And you are the only person you can change.

Step One:

Prayer is essential here. Not just because it's a nice custom to begin everything with prayer, but because you will need God's *revealing* help with your misbeliefs. Ask God to reveal the roots of your own right-person expectations. Ask Him to restore memories you have perhaps spent a lifetime trying to hide from.

Occasionally, someone tells us, "I think I need 'healing of the memories.'" They think it would be nice to have old memories that are painful obliterated by a kind of divine eraser—or touched up a bit by visualized rearrangements of old hurtful scenes from long ago. But I am convinced that forgetting won't make it better. Neither will revising. You need to recall, not forget.

Don't aim to restructure the past into something rosy that never was: Get in touch with it, even if it's very bad. That is the only way you can deal with the erroneous interpretations you developed when you were too young and confused to discern truth. Those meanings that have stayed around to govern and twist your relationships are what you will want to change with the truth. Ask the Holy Spirit to bring accurate recall in His own tender, gentle, careful way. And ask for the courage to tolerate the pain you've been hiding from.

Then pray for healing. Healing of memories does *not* mean changing them so that they are bearable or pleasant. It does *not* mean making up details to add to the past. But God can redeem the past. And He can change its meaning, turning the *consequences* of the past into good. When God heals memories, He uproots erroneous, destructive interpretations or meanings and replaces them with the truth about past events. That truth can set you free. *Effective prayer for healing of memories means prayer for new, truthful meanings and new self-talk to replace old misbeliefs.*

In response to such prayer, God will *reveal* how you interpreted past events to make them utterly traumatic. He will also show how you elaborated their meaning until, like Charlotte, you developed a set of misbeliefs about relationships that have for so long kept you in bondage. He thus prepares you for truth.

Step Two:

Let your mind search the past. Let God take you through your own history, with the object of recalling any events with traumatic effect or significance.

Here we need to say a word or two about psychological traumas. Unlike physical traumas that have an impact on the body, psychological traumas are measured in terms of their meaning. A particular event may be relatively harmless to one person's emotional constitution while another, who interprets the meaning of that event differently, may be injured for life by the very same event. The key to trauma is the individual's interpretation or meaning. Pay attention to what you are telling yourself about an event: how it contributes to your understanding of relationships; what you think it tells you about your value and your significance to others; your goodness and badness; and how good (or bad) you believe God to be. All these are meanings individuals assign to the experiences of life, especially, for our purposes, during childhood.

So you see, as you look at memories, you must remember that events are not stored in our minds as mere happenings, but as happenings *plus* meaning. It's the meaning that makes the difference. For example, one child meets a barking dog and because of his own set of beliefs and ideas, he interprets the situation to mean "The dog is angry at me and is therefore dangerous." Another child encounters the same dog, but having a different set of beliefs, says, "The dog is excited and glad to see me. He's just trying to be friendly."

Another example: A child has a birthday party, to which a certain special friend does not come. Depending on the beliefs that child has acquired, he might say to himself, "My friend doesn't like me, or he would have come to my party." Or, with a different set of beliefs, he might think, "Oh, that's too bad. I'll miss him. He's important to me. But if he says he can't come, I know it must be for a good reason."

I think you can see the point: Trauma may be some childhood occurrence that left deep wounds because of meanings you assigned to it, though others might not have been phased by the same event. So as you search your memory for traumatic events, look for such things as physical or sexual abuse, or various forms of neglect by an adult. Perhaps you will recall being repeatedly castigated verbally or abused emotionally by someone in a primary relationship.

Losses can also be a source of trauma, particularly loss of parental love. Many have grown up unaware that they suffered damage and still experience its consequences from such losses. Did one of your parents, siblings or a close grandparent die during your childhood? The meaning of that loss to you may have left you with right-person misbeliefs. Divorce *always* means loss. All children of divorce suffer damage, no matter how many psychologists their parents hire to make them feel good about the destruction of their homes.[2] Children of missionaries who could not live with their parents for their childhood years, children of alcoholic parents, children of emotionally ill parents, children with a psychotic parent, and children who were somehow exploited by relatives, friends, teachers—all suffer loss.

Destruction of self-esteem through being branded as "trash from the other side of the tracks" by others, picked on and teased, or physically threatened by classmates—this, too, can be traumatic, provided the victim interprets them as catastrophic losses and as having terribly disruptive meanings.

For still others, the loss was only a misinterpretation of the reality situation. For some children conclude that a parent didn't love them contrary to the truth and the facts. Nonetheless, the loss trauma was real.

All such events can have traumatic effect on you and on your relationships today unless God reveals your misbeliefs and the truth to replace them.

---

[2]On this point, see the observations of a popular university professor, Alan Bloom in *The Closing of the American Mind* (New York: Simon and Shuster, 1987).

Charlotte, for example, suffered actual pain from her father's abusive treatment. Even when the physical pains abated, however, she told herself an erroneous *meaning*: "I must be bad, ugly, dirty, repulsive. My father must have a good reason for this. One day my father will love me; if he doesn't, somebody will take his place and fill all my needs, wants and desires." Not one of these notions was warranted.

Why did Charlotte tell herself these things? Why do we make false hypotheses? Perhaps someone else communicated some of this material to Charlotte. But at the bottom, the reason is spiritual: Satan is able to put ideas into human minds. If they're accepted, it's called deception and the result is life-damaging, relationship-wrecking misbeliefs.

So as you search your past, look not only for major events, but even for minor happenings to which you, aided by the enemy, assigned false significance. Record all this carefully in your journal. Remember, do not record only events in your journal, but more important, try to write exhaustively about how you interpreted significant traumas. Recall what you thought about them, what you told yourself, and how you felt.

Step Three.

Forgive. Some recollections may be so upsetting emotionally that forgiveness is impossible for now. *That doesn't matter.* Don't torment yourself when you can't manage to *feel* forgiveness. Just tell God you *do* forgive that person who hurt you. Your feelings will take time to recover. On Jesus' authority, however, you must decide with your will to forgive the persons who hurt you long ago.

While you're forgiving those who have hurt you, you will want to ask God to *reveal* in what ways you might have hurt someone else. If possible, ask forgiveness from those whom you have hurt and do what you can to make it right. Ask and receive God's grace and forgiveness for yourself.

Step Four.

Record your current relationship misbeliefs. One of the best ways to find them is to explore your thoughts in connection with a present friendship or marriage. What kinds of problems come up? What are you telling yourself? When problems arise, get out your journal and write your thoughts and self-talk. Angry? Hurt? Disappointed? Discouraged? Depressed in the context of the relationship? Then without flinching in your honesty, write down what you are telling yourself about the issue. Do you see right-person theories and misbeliefs all over your journal? Do you see expectations of yours being thwarted and dashed?

If you're blinded by a lifelong habit of assuming the problem lies with the other person, you may have trouble identifying your own misbeliefs. It's so tempting to assume you've just gotten involved with the wrong person! We'd like to help you with a "misbelief checklist." Here are some of the ideas that frequently cause trouble in relationships for right-person people. You might locate a number of your own treasured notions:

- There must be a right person somewhere who will love me totally and unconditionally and will meet all my needs.
- Nobody has ever really loved me so far, but the right person will love me devotedly.
- When people get to know me, they don't want me anymore, because none of them so far is the right person.
- The fact that someone hurt me deeply as a child proved to me that I was (and am) bad (or ugly, repulsive, polluted, evil).
- I have so many needs, wants, and hurts that somebody will have to help me, so I'll just wait for that person to come along.
- I expect my friend to (fill the blank) for me, and he doesn't, so I guess he isn't right for me.
- I expect my spouse to (fill the blank) for me, and he doesn't, so I guess he isn't right for me.

- My father (mother) wasn't good to me, [...] someone will someday be the good father [...] never had.
- He never calls me. I always have to call him. Therefore, he isn't the right person.
- My friend got upset with me, so I guess he isn't the right person.
- I don't enjoy sex much, so my spouse must not be the right person for me.
- I got bored with my new friend last night, so I guess he's not the right person for me.
- I need a person who can make me feel good about myself.
- There must be somebody who can make me happy.

Step Five.

Challenge your misbeliefs. Argue against them. And replace them with the truth.

If you want God's *restoring* action to untwist your relationships, you will be *required* to learn to live without fallacies. So, if you have discovered that others often leave you bitter and disappointed, consider what is false about this radical misbelief and its offspring. Look straight at the truth. Here it is:

> *No human being will ever live up to your expectations. No one will ever meet all your needs, or solve all your problems. Nobody will ever love you unconditionally nor relate intimately with you on the basis of utter selflessness. Nobody will ever be able to live for you alone. Nobody will ever manage to care only for your well-being, without giving a thought to his own needs. Nobody!*

Some will argue this point, maybe on religious grounds. "If my husband (wife/friend/child) really loves me as the Bible teaches, I have every right to demand unconditional love and fulfillment! I stand on the Scriptures!"

We have two reasons for insisting that nobody will ever fulfill all your dreams of being perfectly cared for:

1. All men are sinners. And because they are sinners they cannot love perfectly and sinlessly, even if God has commanded them to do so. However saintly and self-giving one may become, he will fail at times with total selflessness.

2. No human being is God. Only God's love is boundless, unconditional, complete and paired with power and resources enough to meet all needs. By contrast, human love at its best is a poor shadow offered by a fellow sinner who himself needs love to keep going. Expecting man to perform as God is such a gross error it's hard to believe anyone would do it. But we do do it and it's time to call a halt.

THE MOST IMPORTANT NEW BELIEF

The Right-Person Theory Is Correct!

We will, as God does His work of *revealing,* courageously face the shattering of the right-person theory because it is a radical misbelief. Replacing your misbeliefs with the truth begins by coming to believe and then learning to tell yourself constantly that Jesus Christ is the Fulfiller of all needs. That's right—*all needs!*

He pointed out to Martha that "one thing is needful"— and that is himself. (See Luke 10:42.) You have absolutely no needs or wants that Jesus cannot and will not either fulfill or (if it isn't right for you) change when the time comes.

He may choose to leave some desires unfulfilled. If He does, the condition will be right for you, and from His refusal you can learn and grow. Rest assured you don't *need* for those desires to be granted, or they would be. Is it painful? Then the pain is right and needful as a condition for learning, growth and refining. When God doesn't change the thoughtlessness of your spouse, doesn't give you a golden child, doesn't send the friend or mate of your dreams, doesn't anesthetize your psychic distress, tell yourself the absolute truth without flinching or dodging it:

The Right Person is in charge of my life. Not one thing is other than He would have it—and that is precisely what I need. He loves me and meets my needs completely.

With this belief firmly planted in your internal monologue, you can handle it when others fail to live up to your expectations, or when the people God actually gives you don't measure up to your dreams and fantasies.

And you can roll up your sleeves and put into your relationships the same love with which God has loved you.

SEVEN

Jealousy

Jealousy, like milk gone sour, can spoil even the best of relationships. It robs friendships of their comfort, drains meaning from marriages, supplants understanding with confusion. It can keep you awake, make your digestive tract twist, and mash your will to mush. It can beget murderous hatred!

GLORIA AND LORIN

To arrive at a definition of jealousy, we will look in on Gloria and Lorin. Lorin is a clergyman. Gloria and Lorin have two small children. Here they are telling their counselor about their difficulties:

Gloria: We're so unhappy. I don't think Lorin understands my needs at all. He tells me he loves me, but his actions don't show it.

Lorin: I know what she means by that! She thinks I should never want to do a single thing without her; that's what she means. She gets upset with me because I want to play golf once in a while on Saturday afternoons.

Gloria: It's not only your Saturday golf games, Lorin! Tell him how you stay away from home every Monday night by having a meeting with the stewardship committee. And Tuesday nights—they're supposed to be free, but last Tuesday you said you had to make calls on people who aren't home in the daytime. There's a midweek service on Wednesday. Thursdays you're always at council meetings. Lorin, *you're never home!*

Lorin: It's not that bad. Sure, this week I was gone a little more than usual, but I'm almost always home Tuesday nights. And I make a point of taking Monday off for Gloria. We even went on a picnic with the kids last Monday.

Gloria: And what happened at the park? I'm glad you brought that up! Tell the doctor what you did during our so-called "family" picnic! You met Marianne and the two of you had one of your "nice chats" while I watched the kids. Marianne was enrapt, of course, finding you at the park without your usual waiting line of admirers. And what's worse, you were enthralled! You paid more attention to her than you ever pay to your family. It's the same old story.

Lorin: For heaven's sake! What am I supposed to do? Ignore people? Marianne is one of our church members. I can't tell her to drop dead! No matter how hard I try to please Gloria, she gets upset if I have anything to do with other people.

The counselor didn't have to say much to keep this interview going. Had he allowed it, Gloria and Lorin would have escalated their argument until she burst into tears and he lost his temper, the usual course of their quarrels at home. The counselor later discovered Lorin's need for universal approval and recognition, driven by deep misbeliefs about personal incompetence. Gloria's jealousy wasn't the couple's only problem. But for now, let's take a closer look at the jealousy component in the couple's shared misery.

Here is Gloria's misbelief:

I am losing something that is mine by virtue of

marriage and motherhood, namely Lorin's love; I am losing my rightful share of his time and attention. Furthermore, I must have large portions of Lorin's time and attention to survive.

Gloria's beliefs can help us understand what jealousy is: namely, the perception that one is losing, or has lost something of crucial importance.

Whenever jealousy creeps into a relationship, the jealous person believes these three things:

- I am losing someone's attention, concern, affection, or something else that is rightfully mine.
- What I am losing is so valuable to me I *must* keep it.
- What I am losing is going to another person or to another concern.

Gloria's jealousy, based on these beliefs, was twisting her marriage.

THE ROOTS OF GLORIA'S JEALOUSY

For Gloria's restoration, God began His gracious work of *revealing*. As she probed her history with the counselor, she uncovered the roots of her radical jealousy misbelief.

Gloria was three when her sister, Joy, was born. The baby arrived with a physical anomaly, requiring repeated surgery during the first three years of her life. The baby needed especially large doses of care and love, so she received the tenderness and parental attention little Gloria had come to regard as rightfully hers.

To the mind of the toddler, the infant was an intruder, robbing her of all that had made life sweet and secure. Her parents understood Gloria's feelings of deprivation, and they tried to make up for them by giving her extra attention, but Joy's needs were massive. Gloria's childish reasoning accounted for her parents' absences by developing a hypothesis destined many years later to carve a jagged scar on her union with Lorin.

Here is Gloria's original hypothesis:

I am not lovable, and that's why my parents leave me alone to be with Joy. I'll never be as lovable as someone sick or in need.

This theory seemed to Gloria to be confirmed by her days and hours with sitters while her parents watched by her sister's hospital bed. Later, Gloria's hypothesis developed into a general rule of life:

I must always be careful, or those who love me will be taken by someone in need and I'll be left alone again.

Gloria applied her hypothesis to her later relationships and in the process, her radical misbelief grew even stronger. She relied on her theory to interpret events in her early play relationships and later friendships, only to find that it was a self-confirming belief.

Adolescence was stormy and miserable for her, and her dating relationships were marred and shortened by her jealous fears. These sad results were in turn taken by Gloria as evidence of the validity of her theory. Because her belief in eventual loss affected her actions, she often drove away, with her jealousy, the very people she feared losing the most. And because she saw her relationships through this jealousy misbelief as through tinted spectacles, she made it impossible for herself to feel secure in the love of another. She doused the fires of others' caring. Her fear, hurt and anger led her to burden friendships with suspicion and demands.

MANY PEOPLE FEEL SOME JEALOUSY

To the extent that you find this foundational misbelief in yourself, you may discover that you, too, began in early life to view someone else—most likely a sibling, perhaps a playmate, or even a parent who acted like a child—as a rival. Rivalry between siblings furnishes many occasions for misbeliefs to grow in the mind of a child.

The better you know the Scriptures, the less you will be shocked to discover your own jealousies, because you will be aware that you were born fallen and that sinners can be deceived by Satan, even as children. You may be able to recall something in your history that will account to your satisfaction for your own jealousy. If you can, it should help you to understand your radical jealousy misbelief better and deal with it more effectively.

The jealous person believes:

I always lose what means the most to me; so I am losing (will lose/have lost) this time, too, and I can't stand losing again.

On the basis of this *radical misbelief,* the jealous person usually construes the behavior of others to mean he is "one down," even when he's not. Eventually, in any significant relationship, he comes to believe he is losing. He studies the actions of others through the lenses of his misbelief, so his view is distorted by it. Usually, it is his misbelief that makes ordinary actions by another appear to mean loss of love.

Gloria, for instance, could not see her marriage except through the distorting lenses of her radical misbelief. Her husband had no romantic interest in anyone else, nor had he yet lost his love for Gloria. But because of her beliefs, she saw a twisted version of reality, one by which her marriage might eventually be ruined.

DETECTING YOUR OWN JEALOUSY

We don't like to see ourselves as jealous. So we need scrupulous honesty to detect our own tendencies in this direction. Because jealousy can dynamite otherwise fine relationships, it's imperative to find and correct the rumblings of jealousy in ourselves.

The following are some of the characteristics through which jealousy shows itself.

Unhappy in relationships. If you are frequently misera-

ble in romantic, marital, or friendly relationshi
jealousy as a possible cause. You keep yoursel:
because you believe you are losing, or will ever
your friend or loved one to someone else. You might keep
yourself anxious, sleepless and irritable as well and for similar reasons.

Possessive, overprotective. Do friends and loved ones complain that you stifle them, don't give them space, crowd
them? Do they resent your frequent anger when they want
to do something without you? Do you make their decisions
for them and foist your opinions on them? Do you get upset
when they don't buy what you buy, read what you read, and
like what you like? Does it bother you when those you love
"do their own thing"? You may be taking all these perfectly
normal signs of personal integrity as evidence that you are
losing love again. Your efforts at controlling them are attempts to hang on, but they will backfire.

Suspicious, watchful. Do you check up on those you love?
Do you often suspect that they are relating to others when
you aren't looking, caring more for someone else than for
you, replacing you with someone or something else? Do you
have trouble trusting others to truly care about your well-
being or to keep on loving you? Do you seem to have to be
watchful, constantly on the alert to guard against losing?
Do you often ask questions to try to feel the other person out
to see if you have been betrayed or if you are being shoved
aside emotionally? Are you so watchful, tense, and suspicious that you can hardly ever relax and enjoy another person? So attentive to what every single behavioral nuance
"means" you can't feel good when you're with your friend or
loved one? Have you been called *paranoid*?

When you ask questions to allay your suspicions, you
usually find the answers unsatisfactory. You are sure your
friends talk about you behind your back, your spouse flirts
with others when you aren't looking. You wonder if others
respect you. It occurs to you that they might actually snicker
when you aren't watching them, joke about you to each

other. Or you may think others mean to do you harm, and you expect them to try to take advantage of you sooner or later. You have little faith in the goodwill of others toward you. Sometimes, suspicious jealousy even makes relationships so strenuous, you might unconsciously wreck them yourself rather than endure the strain.

Angry, irritable. Do you get angry in relationships because your self-talk assures you others mean to rip you off? Do friends seem puzzled and alienated by your anger?

You may show hurt, tearful, crabby, fault-finding attitudes and actions, even in extreme cases harming another person. Or you may vengefully break off a friendship or pursue a divorce.

Angry in your jealousy, you may pretend you don't care, or flaunt other friendships where you're sure your loved one will see, hoping to make them jealous, too. You may try to get even by having an affair and making sure you're found out.

You believe that you're *entitled* to that love you think you're losing. It's yours by rights! And it's terrible and wrong that you're being deprived. Somebody should pay dearly for hurting you!

Sad to say, you can and will cause your dire predictions to come true by your own cranky irritability. So people who begin by loving you leave you alone until you really do lose them.

"Loving." Another way to be jealous is to pour on the fake love. You try harder to prevent loss of love. You redouble your effort, pull out all the stops, exert yourself to be "nice" to the point where the other feels under pressure, trapped, and even manipulated. Others interpret your excessive effort as a demand to perform! Your words and actions seem to them an obvious prompting: "Act like I do—show your love for me with souped-up enthusiasm."

You say, "I love *you!*" too often and with a slight upward inflection that translates into: "Say 'I love you' to me, and say it as passionately as I do!"

You pour it on because you think you're losing, doing the things the other person wished you'd done earlier in the relationship. You make it very obvious that you're trying to manipulate. You think that if you can only act loving enough, you'll make the other person express more love to you and then you can believe again you're not losing.

This "loving" jealousy puts pressure on relationships, pressure others resent and resist. Furthermore, no matter how much effort the other person expends to express love, you will never be truly satisfied until your radical jealousy misbelief is corrected by the truth.

Passivity. Believing you are losing love, you stop all effort at relating and become passive in the relationship.

You now avoid the friend or loved one and do absolutely nothing to revive the friendship or contribute anything to it emotionally. Peeved or sad, you wait for the other person to do something effective. You might be silent, refusing to talk. Or you might make it obvious that you're keeping your conversation on a superficial plane so the other person knows you are withholding intimacy.

You tell yourself you lose no matter how hard you try, so you might as well give up. Nothing you do ever helps anyway. It's awful to be so helpless, you think, awful to lose again. But you just can't believe anything you might try would help at all.

This one is especially hard to break, because others frequently meet it by trying harder. And so they reward you for being so sullen. Sad to say, this will only increase the likelihood that you'll sulk again when things get rough. What's so bad about that? Eventually, the other person will tire of expending effort without permanent improvement, and you will have ruined a relationship with your passive jealousy.

How many of your own habitual attitudes and actions did you find in these descriptions of various pathways for jealousy? Careful self-searching is worthwhile because of the negative effect of jealousy on friendships.

WHAT JEALOUSY DOES TO RELATIONSHIPS

Jealousy cannot produce constructive results. The jealous person, at some level, is ashamed of his own behavior, while the other person gets tired of trying to defend himself against false accusations.

At first, the other person will probably try to argue that the fear of loss is unfounded and that there is nothing to be jealous about. He may then make a special effort to demonstrate caring in order to convince the jealous person that his fear of loss is unfounded. Because jealousy is not allayed by efforts at reassurance, such efforts will usually reinforce the jealousy. A period of temporary relief will be followed by a return of jealous behavior. Now it is *more frequent* and *more intense* because the other has rewarded it with efforts to reassure. The relationship will become hostage to jealousy until it is ruined.

Are you the jealous person in relationships? Do you yearn for lasting friendships, intimacy and enduring love, but fail in relationships? You will never read anything more important for your search than the previous paragraph. Read it again and try to review in your mind how your jealousy has milked reassurance from others. Though you felt temporarily as though harmony and rapport were restored, you turned out to be utterly wrong. You became jealous again all too soon. And though you may have blamed the other person, the inevitable result of your jealous actions must be devastation! Your loved one will become discouraged and even irritated. A conviction of helplessness will replace his caring. He will learn eventually that nothing he does can cure your jealousy. You will *cause* that which you fear.

But you can learn another way, if you choose.

Others of you may find yourself the object of jealousy. If so, and if you are beginning to despair of ever filling that bottomless pit of demand for reassurance and demonstrations of loyalty, your script in the drama of cure requires that you *stop reassuring*. You only water and feed the jealousy by producing jealousy-cued expressions of undying love, faithful friendship, utter fealty; excessive and unreasonable demonstrations on demand of your utter commitment. Tell the jealous one he must work on his own jealousy by replacing the jealous misbeliefs with the security-restoring truth.

HOW TO CURE JEALOUSY: THE JEALOUS PERSON

Let's return to Gloria, joining her in a session with her counselor. Since the Lord not only *reveals* but *requires* that we work to understand, the counselor wants to help Gloria develop insight into her jealousy as well as a sense of personal responsibility for it.

Counselor: Have you thought more about how you get upset with Lorin? What happens between the two of you to generate your bad feelings?

Gloria: Yes, I have thought about that. Usually, I'll start feeling neglected because he isn't giving me the attention I need. When he leaves me alone to go play golf or chat with somebody else after he's been gone so much, I feel as if he doesn't care—doesn't love me—and I get upset. I usually show my feelings, even when I try not to. And then . . .

Counselor: And then?

Gloria: Well, I was just thinking. It's like when I was little. My mom and dad, you know. When my sister, Joy, came, they—it used to upset me how they'd ignore me and pick Joy up. Play with her. And they never knew. They never knew how—what I was feeling. How hurt I was. But Lorin knows. I let him know. So why doesn't he change? Why can't I—why can't he make some adjustments?

Counselor: Do you think your parents would have changed—would have spent less time and effort

	with Joy—if they had known how hurt you were?
Gloria:	I guess so. They probably would have tried. But—maybe they couldn't. You know what I mean? I think they would have felt bad if they'd known how I felt, and they might have tried to explain more. But they still wouldn't have been able to do less for Joy. She needed lots of care, with her handicap. Now, as I look back, I guess they probably *wanted* to give me the attention I needed. They just couldn't do it. I know they loved me.
Counselor:	But when you were little, you thought perhaps they didn't love you as much, because you felt ignored in favor of Joy?
Gloria:	I must have thought they didn't love me, maybe because I wasn't lovable.
Counselor:	You believed you were losing something you had a right to keep. Trying to figure it out, you concluded you must be less lovable than Joy. After all, she was getting what you were losing.
Gloria:	That's right. I'm sure I must have believed I was losing everything important. And I must have assumed something was wrong with me—something about me was not very attractive, maybe.
Counselor:	And you now know that what you believed was not true?
Gloria:	Well, I know my parents loved me and wanted to give me care and attention. But—I wonder if I really know, deep down, that I'm not unattractive or unlovable?

What is amazing is that even a toddler constructs theories about relationships. Little Gloria had worked on finding meaning in events. And she created a meaning of her own whereby she could understand what was happening in her primary relationships. Of course, she could not have spelled it out as succinctly as this, but here is Gloria's old radical relationship misbelief as it manifested itself in her counseling:

> *I am losing the love of my parents because I am not lovable; not being lovable, I will never be sure of being loved. I will probably lose the love that is rightfully mine whenever somebody like Joy comes along.*

Gloria's misbelief, applied in full force to her relationship with Lorin, amounted to the jealousy misbelief. Notice how:

- The misbelief was developed early by Gloria in the context of her primary relationships.
- Gloria had chosen to marry a clergyman. Could she have been drawn to him because clergymen are supposed to be caring, loving, nurturing people? If so, her choice of a spouse might have been an unconscious effort to ensure that she would be loved in spite of her radical misbelief.
- However, Gloria's relationship with Lorin only reactivated her radical relationship misbelief. Her clergyman-husband *did* have a strong need to nurture, but the nature of his profession led to his giving care and attention liberally to members of his parish. Gloria's unconscious selection had therefore backfired.
- To Gloria, operating from the perspective of her radical misbelief, life was handing her a cruel repetition of the terrible loss she had felt in childhood. Not only did she believe she was losing what was rightfully hers, but the only explanation she had ever come up with seemed to apply: She must be unlovable.

MISINTERPRETING LOVE

Like most love-jealous people, Gloria misinterpreted the word love and misconstrued the meaning of other people's (specifically Lorin's) actions.

As we worked together, she came to understand that, as

a toddler, she had had no resources for understanding the word love in any way other than as a synonym for parental attention: *Love = attention.* Gloria took this to be a truth so basic it needed no examination. It meant that the amount of love someone has for you is directly proportional to the amount of attention that person pays to you.

Like other love-jealous adults, she perpetuated her misbelief into adulthood, childishly telling herself that Lorin's attention to any of his parishioners was robbing her of love.

QUESTION YOUR EQUATIONS

As it became clear that God was *requiring* Gloria's active participation in finding the truth, the counselor encouraged her to question her equation of love with attention. Jealous people need to question their equations. ("Why am I so sure love means attention?")

Gloria was able to look at facts and to question her old conclusions until it dawned on her that mature love can flourish even when people don't give each other as much time and attention as they devote to other concerns. She was shocked when she considered the fact that her parents clearly loved each other, even after she and her sister began to require most of their time and attention. She had never before even considered the question, but had no doubt that their love did not cease when they could no longer focus large amounts of time on one another. She admitted, reluctantly, that a person's attention might be claimed first by duty, either parental or (Gloria reluctantly admitted) pastoral.

You see, God *requires* personal effort. For Gloria, working all this through took a great deal of time and effort. At last Gloria's understanding of the truth widened to include new and liberating awareness: There was no question that she had been loved always; love was something different from attention, consideration, concern and focus; and she could count on Lorin's love even when his attention was riveted on some needy parishioner.

Now, through the truth, the Lord began *restoring* what had been damaged by jealousy. Gloria was able to give up her *love = attention* equation. She also became free to make requests of Lorin without fear of loss of love. She asked him to build some walls around his home life and arrange to give more attention to his wife and family unadulterated by interruptions from parish concerns. Lorin agreed.

All this took time, prayer and effort. What can be described in six paragraphs or less, reading like a spectacular therapeutic triumph, goes slowly and haltingly in practice. There were setbacks and difficulties.

For example, Lorin kept breaking his agreements. He continued to treat even the smallest requests of his parishioners as emergencies and rushed to deal with them, riding roughshod over promises to set aside time for the family. It was a major breakthrough when he finally grasped the fact that every request for his pastoral presence did *not* constitute an emergency, and that he did not need to keep proving his worth to himself by responding as if people couldn't make a move without his immediate involvement. All this is easy to read on a page of type, but not so easy for countless deeply involved Christian pastors to live by.

Gloria had to put up with bouts of resentment, anger and despair. Her hardest task was to work relentlessly at changing what she told herself whether Lorin kept his part of the bargain or not. She had to develop the habit of accurate diagnosis, learning to tell herself:

> *The problem is not Lorin's involvement with the finance committee, but my misbelief. It is nonsense to tell myself that I'm losing Lorin's love! To a finance committee? I've got to be kidding! My problem is my belief that if Lorin isn't constantly reassuring me with attention, he doesn't love me!*

Gloria practiced telling herself the new truth she had come to grasp and understand:

Love does not equal attention. Lorin's activities are his problem. My feelings are my problem. I don't have to be upset because he is paying attention to something else. I don't have to have his attention every instant, and I refuse to keep on equating attention with love.

By directly countering her jealousy misbeliefs, Gloria was able to experience the freeing power of the truth and to maintain, with increasing satisfaction, the sense of security obtained from no longer needing to believe she wasn't lovable.

NOT ALL JEALOUSY IS OVER LOVE

While the jealous person always believes he is losing, or will lose something that is rightfully his, the issue is not always loss of love.

Clark is jealous over the time Lee spends with the boss; Marcia thinks Alice is trying to take her place as president of the league—and it worries her; Carol is threatened by the new girl who might displace her as the class beauty; Mark finds himself worrying because Todd has been offering powerful prayers in Bible class, prayers that might be better than Mark's.

The jealous person may fear someone else's co-opting his power, fame, wealth, honor, prestige, reputation, preeminence, even spiritual gifts. Since almost anything can be lost to someone else, any good thing can become a source of misery.

I want to point out clearly that sometimes jealousy occurs in reaction to real losses as well as imagined ones. Occasionally the jealous person actually does lose someone's love, the loyalty of an employee, the fame he has come to depend on, or the status he has counted so important. It actually does happen that someone else gets what we have considered vital to our interests. When the loss is real, it is not a misbelief. But the deeper misbeliefs of jealousy remain erroneous, even when the loss actually occurs.

What makes jealousy deadly to the jealous person is the deeply held belief that the love or fame or wealth or loyalty or whatever he has come to depend on is *irrevocably his and he must have it, indeed, very likely cannot survive without it.* This belief that the thing being lost is an essential—that without it one can never have peace or happiness, that one would be incomplete if it were lost, that continued existence would be impossible or at least worthless, that it is of such crucial importance that everything depends on continuing to possess it—this belief is what leads jealous people to murder and suicide, acts of revenge and destruction.

Not only is this belief false, it is most destructive. If you harbor it, you must challenge it, root it out, battle it until it's dead, and replace it with the truth. Not only because it is a misery-generating notion but because *it is the misbelief of idolatry,* the misbelief that something created holds the place of God. The truth is that only God, revealed uniquely in Jesus Christ, is essential, crucial, and absolutely necessary for life to be worthwhile.

This truth is the truth of the first of all commandments. Transmuted from imperative to indicative, this commandment reveals the pearl of great price: The only object worth loving with all your heart, soul, and mind so that you cannot afford to lose it or have it taken from you is God himself. Having Him at the center, even the loss of life itself can be borne.

HOW TO DEAL WITH YOUR OWN JEALOUSY

First, accept responsibility for your jealousy. Most jealous people project the problem, as Gloria did, onto the behavior of someone else. She blamed her hurt feelings on Lorin's choices. When you are jealous, you will wrongly see the problem as due to someone else's *taking* something from you, something that is so rightfully yours that the other person becomes, in your eyes, villainous.

Whatever other people may be up to, your jealousy is *your* behavior. It results from certain beliefs, feelings and actions of your own. Unless you are prepared to take it as axiomatic that your behavior is *your* responsibility, you will not change, but will go on expecting others to do something about your hurt feelings.

This insight doesn't necessarily exonerate anyone else or declare anyone else utterly free from responsibility. Other people are responsible for their own choices and actions, too. But it does put your jealousy in the only place where you can do something about it: right at your door. Your jealousy is *your* responsibility.

Second, carefully analyze your jealousy. As you pray for God's gracious *revealing,* write your analysis in your journal. Jealousy occurs as a process with four distinguishable components. Let's look at them briefly.

Component #1 is an event or a situation that serves as a trigger for the jealousy process to occur. In Gloria's case it was usually some unexpected action of Lorin's in response to parishioners' claims on him. A chance remark by someone, a glance, the expression of someone's face, another person's bragging or flaunting of something you have considered yourself to have a corner on—many, many kinds of events can be triggers. Discover what happened to trigger your current bout of jealousy. Note the triggering event in your journal.

Component #2 is your perception (right or wrong) of the event as signalling loss of something valuable and rightfully yours, to some other person, concern, or issue. Discern how you are telling yourself: "I am losing something. Since it is mine and I need it and must have it, this loss is intolerable and awful." Log this self-talk.

Component #3 is a batch of resultant autonomic nervous system responses to your interpretations and beliefs described in #2. We call this batch of events *emotional arousal*. Because of what you're telling yourself, you experience unpleasant emotional arousal in the form of hurt, frustration, anger, anxiety and/or depression. Write a description of your feelings.

Component #4 is overt behavior. You *act* jealous. You cry, you lecture, you rage, you tighten your lips, you refuse to talk, you look and act melancholy. Actions or overt behavior, intentional or unintentional, will occur sooner or later, no matter how much you may try to hide your jealousy. In extreme cases, jealousy leads to homicidal actions. In Gloria, it led to nagging, crying and complaining. Among other possibilities, jealousy can hurt so badly that one seeks help for the problem as Gloria did. Make a note of your jealous behavior.

With the help of God's work of *revealing,* analyze your own jealousy. As you write out your own jealousy components, note and journal in detail the elements in #2. "What am I telling myself about this situation?" Ask the Lord, and record the thoughts you get in answer to it. As you seek the truth, God will reveal it.

Third, remembering that God requires change, look at your notes and locate what you may be able to change. Usually, the jealous person has exhausted himself trying to change the situation, the other persons involved, the circumstances. It is not inconceivable that we can occasionally solve the problem by modifying circumstances. Not very often, however, since, for the most part, harmful jealousy is a problem *in us,* not in the circumstances of our lives.

Most often, you will discover the most fruitful component for change is #2. Thoughtfully study your written-out self-talk. Discover your radical jealousy misbelief and your current jealousy misbeliefs related to it. Now research your beliefs in the light of Scripture, the facts, this chapter, and maybe some conversations with wise counselors or friends. Take all this to God, asking for the illumination of the Holy Spirit. Give yourself plenty of quiet time to think and pray that God will *reveal* to you how you acquired your radical jealousy misbelief. Use your Spirit-enlightened reason to find and challenge the falsehoods in your erroneous perceptions, interpretations and assumptions, and replace them with the truth. Notice and apply truth at every level. But whatever you do, study and work with the major truth taught by the First Commandment, *Thou shalt have no other gods before me.* Note your truth discoveries in your journal.

We can count on the power of the Holy Spirit to help us change, for He empowers what He requires.

Fourth, you have the power to modify your overt behavior, at least to some extent. If your jealousy has led to sinful actions toward others, which are nagging, complaining, rejecting, withdrawn and silent, or otherwise hurtful, plain ordinary good judgment ought to tell you that such behavior in the face of perceived loss of love can only result in further alienation of the very love you want to hang on to. And even if it doesn't alienate anyone else, it will result in a negative self-evaluation and more bad feelings when you yourself face up to the way you've been acting.

Naturally, when Gloria began acting less miserable over Lorin's absences, Lorin found her more attractive to be around. This might serve as a rule of thumb for those given to jealous behavior. Changing your sullen anger, your vindictive attempts to get even and your bitter speech, and replacing them with loving behavior may make you more attractive to others. Whether it does that or not, it will help heal your pain.

Don't try to force change in component #3. Attempts to force oneself to feel different without changing self-talk and misbeliefs result in nothing but frustration, denial of one's real feelings and considerable indirect emotional backfiring. This component will change automatically when you have truth in your self-talk.

Your attempts to change component #1, circumstances, have probably proved rather fruitless. Generally, some change in circumstances is possible, but it's much better to attempt this *after* you have left jealousy behind you. Then it may be time to ask others to work with you to improve circumstances.

As God *reveals* your jealousy and its misbeliefs, and you participate in change as He *requires*, He will *restore* precious relationships. The truth makes free, according to Jesus himself. This means your relationships can be free from the eroding of jealousy, and others can be set free to love you. Best of all, *you* can be free from the anguish of a jealous heart.

EIGHT

People-Pleasers

Unless you are completely lacking in manners, you are bound to be a people-pleaser, to some extent.

The very idea of a person who *never* gives a thought to pleasing anybody seems far-fetched. Picture a three-year-old who tore up our clinic waiting room. He never gave a thought to pleasing anybody, it appeared. First, the ambitious little fellow threw *all* the magazines on the floor. He refused to pick them up. When his embarrassed mother reached out to restrain him, he slapped her and wrenched himself away. The poor, haggard woman was reduced to begging. It got her nowhere! She ordered him to come and sit down with her. The toddler responded, "No! You can't make me!" Our receptionist smiled at him. Though her smile softens the hardest heart, the child stuck out his tongue. A counselor came to help, knelt beside the boy—and was kicked in the stomach.

It was a good thing this was a little boy. An adult with a similar behavior pattern would find himself in a cell. Adults *have to* please others to live a normal life.

The problem is, some of us go too far. The people-pleasers make pleasing the end and aim of life. They pay a price, however, for their excessive pleasing twists nearly all of their relationships.

Take Judy, for instance. We are not telling Judy's story

as an example of what all people-pleasers are like. They don't come from the same pod like identical peas. Your history of people-pleasing may be different. But to the extent that you, too, are an inveterate people-pleaser, you'll find in Judy some traits matching your own.

Judy's story can help you find and identify your people-pleasing misbeliefs.

Everyone liked Judy. She was so agreeable, always going out of her way to do what others expected—and more, if she could.

Her large, blue eyes were wide, reflecting pristine innocence. One glance assured you of her amiable acceptance. You just knew she would never be irritated, never cross.

This tall honey blonde, twenty-five years of age, and full of energy, would have caught anyone's eye. But it was not her looks that captivated; it was the sweetness of her nature. Here was a person who always managed to put the wishes of others first. She believed her compliance was Christian love in action, though she rarely thought about such things. Most of her friends, too, ascribed her goodness to selfless living out of the biblical imperative to "love your neighbor as yourself."

Judy had called her friend at 11:30 one night when she realized she couldn't finish making favors for the mother-daughter banquet. She'd promised they'd be ready by the next morning and she'd tried her best. Her friend had sounded irritated. When Judy hung up, she burst into tears. Couldn't anyone *ever* understand that she was only one person—not a committee? She'd just have to try harder. Fresh tears brimmed over the red rims of her tired eyes, and Judy's despairing sobs punctuated the early morning quiet.

Why was she so upset over such a minor thing, she agonized, when a worse event left her totally unmoved?

When Judy came for Christian counseling, her wide-eyed sweetness showed like a trademark. Under the sweetness, a thick layer of repressed, negative emotion churned, strewing wreckage throughout Judy's relationships.

This compliant young mother informed her counselor, through tears, that she had recently been seduced by an older woman. The sweet "I'll-do-anything-for-you" nature made such an event predictable. Though Judy was a Christian for whom sexual morality had always been habitual, a compliant nature made it easy for the seducer to convince her that their affair was "special" and even scriptural. Judy's buried motives had exerted their own pressure.

When asked how she had allowed such an aberration, all Judy could say was, "I don't know."

Moreover, she was puzzled by a lack of guilt feelings after the encounter. Her absence of feelings had even begun to frighten her. She comprehended, rightly, that she ought to have strong feelings about the sexual misadventure. Where had her emotions gone? Why, when others were furious at the seducer, did Judy herself feel only emptiness? This strange inability to feel alarmed Judy, and had prompted her to seek Christian counseling.

"What's wrong with me?" she sobbed. "Why doesn't my behavior make sense? Why can't I feel? Does anyone else ever ask questions like these? Am I sick? Will I get better?"

Though hesitant, Judy ventured, with the counselor's help, to bring to light some long-forgotten scenes. The counselor encouraged Judy to search for early-formed beliefs by exploring primary relationships.

As the Lord performed His perfect work of *revealing*, Judy saw herself at age eight, standing perplexed over her alcoholic mother who was crumpled and unconscious on the living room floor. Daddy was out of town on a business trip—again. It was up to Judy, as the oldest child, to take care of the family. On her shoulders rested the duty of stuffing Mother back into bed and seeing that little brother and sister were fed, bathed and loved.

"If Daddy comes home before I get it all done, he'll yell and scream!" she thought. "Or even worse, he'll have that sadness in his face. If I do everything right, I can make Mommy feel better, keep Daddy happy, and keep Rickie and Tammy quiet, too."

Judy's life started to make sense. Her counselor pointed out that, even at the tender age of eight, Judy had formulated a hypothesis to make sense of relationships.

Every child feels a fundamental entitlement to love, care and protection. When these are not provided by adults, the world falls apart. It seemed obvious to Judy, at eight years old, that her worth depended on making others happy. For her to have value, she believed, it was vital to take care of everything for everybody, to go to any lengths to right whatever was wrong. Wasn't this the only explanation for the fact that, unless she could manage everything right, the earth caved in under the whole family? Her daddy had even told her how much he expected of his "big girl."

Whenever Judy felt abandoned, she puzzled over the meaning of her parents' behavior. "Why would Mommy rather drink than take care of me? Why doesn't Daddy come home and straighten all this out?" But that would mean more fighting, and that was the most terrible thing of all. She hated the yelling, screaming, kicking and biting more than anything in the world. Maybe she should try harder—if she could only be good enough and handle everything better, maybe they wouldn't have anything to fight about, maybe Mommy would stop drinking and Daddy would stay home.

All this, Judy had put out of consciousness with parental assistance. Burying pain helped her not to feel it. Judy's father also denied reality by refusing to discuss the family tragedy. So Judy came to believe she'd better ignore it all, too—never rock the boat, never say anything to upset Mom or Dad; just figure out what everyone expects and do it. Meanwhile, Mother's drinking taught little Judy a pathological lesson about how painful feelings could be drowned.

Along with God's revelation of memories, something else returned. Judy felt inner pain she hadn't known existed. She could *feel* after all. And she could grasp the reasons for the pain. She discovered that beliefs she had learned long ago had determined her behavior in relationships. Judy had cooperated in being exploited! Such fear of abandonment had governed thoughts and actions that Judy gave her all, questioned nothing, and let herself be trampled over at anyone's whim.

Judy realized now she had barely noticed the psychological beating she'd received from her drug-abusing former husband. While Judy worked to earn income and struggled to hold the family together, Ed had bought himself toys—cars, trucks, motorcycles, women—complaining loudly if she spent five dollars for a magazine subscription. She had taken his complaints seriously and tried harder to please him. He had taken advantage of her compliance in every conceivable way.

Judy also realized that friends had frequently used her, considering this sweet young woman extraordinarily gifted with mercy for their benefit. Since she never complained, they naturally believed she didn't mind when others exploited her good nature. How clear it now appeared that the seduction had only been the most dramatic of many rip-offs!

Now that God had revealed to Judy the childhood roots of her misery, as well as the negative aspects of her current relationships, it was time to look at the connection between *then* and *now*. Why was an adult woman acting maladaptively without any more insight than an eight-year-old?

JUDY'S RADICAL RELATIONSHIP MISBELIEF

Working from their reconstruction of Judy's early theorizing about her interactions with family members, she and her counselor examined each of Judy's present relationships. In all of them, Judy had been operating with her old "I have to please everybody" hypothesis. Working to weaken all her human connections was Judy's radical relationship misbelief. She put it into words like this:

> *I must make everything right for everyone, absolutely never displeasing anybody. Anything I might*

think or do that wouldn't please everybody is utterly unacceptable.

Based on her early devised misbelief, Judy was firmly convinced

- I mustn't even think of not pleasing anyone.
- Even my feelings must be socially acceptable, and I must not have emotions that anybody would disapprove of.
- I must be adequate at all times to meet all requests, demands, and needs, making everything nice for everybody.
- If I fail anyone, displease anyone, or upset anyone, my world will collapse in a way too dreadful to think about.

These erroneous beliefs, based on thinking as a child (St. Paul's words from 1 Corinthians 13), were the direct cause of Judy's present relationship failures.

GOD'S REVEALING, REQUIRING AND RESTORATION

After the Lord began to reveal, Judy came to understand what He required of her: She was required now to will to find the truth and substitute it for the radical misbelief and its spin-offs. God illuminated for her the words of David in Psalm 51, "Thou desirest truth in the inward being, therefore teach me wisdom in my secret heart."

When she was willing to be whole, willing to replace her misbeliefs with true precepts, Judy knew God's work of restoration. She was empowered by the Spirit of God with courage to follow through what God had begun. Her steps of recovery involved:

- making an energetic effort to change her childish thinking to adult thinking by discussing her feelings and misbeliefs with her counselor, thinking through what she felt and what she was telling herself;
- keeping a journal and recording her feelings and reactions during daily interactions with others, noting

especially her self-talk and working to discover the misbeliefs in it, replacing them with the truth;

- scheduling a time daily for doing something for reasons of her own, something that would achieve goals she felt God had given *her*, regardless of whether others would be pleased or not;
- struggling hard not to take responsibility for her friends' and her family's problems.

The habit of automatically reacting to make others feel better did not give way easily or comfortably, and Judy's acquaintances and loved ones had come to expect her to handle whatever they dumped on her, so Judy had to force herself to stop and think when people made requests. She tried to actually disagree with someone or confront an issue each day—a brand new behavior. Here, Judy made every effort to distinguish carefully between her duty to love others (which she wanted to do) and her habit of being their puppet—a distinction she often found difficult. All this required extreme discipline, but Judy began to feel less guilt as she developed greater self-control.

As Judy succeeded in telling herself the truth and walking in that truth, God's work of restoration became obvious to her. A new calm settled over the household. The tension that once drove Judy was replaced with serenity. The children, seeing a change in their mother, changed their own behavior. Judy found her fear of conflict diminishing, and discovered she could survive quite well if someone became irritated with her for a time.

The most rewarding outcome of all was her new relationship with the family Judy once feared. The Lord had been working in Judy's parents' lives, too. As she became open, honest and expressive, Judy's mother (now in recovery from her alcoholism) and father responded in kind. So relationships changed and improved. The once unspoken rules: *don't talk, don't feel, don't trust* were replaced with *please show me who you really are, how you really feel, and how*

*well you understand. I won't abandon or reject you for your
feelings.*

"It was hard work, but it was worth it," Judy confided to
her counselor during one of their sessions together. "I have
discovered what Jesus wanted to do in me when He showed
me His Word, 'You shall know the truth, and the truth shall
make you free'! God really has revealed that truth, required
some difficult changes, and restored my damaged relationships!"

"I CAN'T BE HAPPY IF . . ."

Are your relationships twisted by people-pleasing? Do
you recognize yourself in these words?

I can't be happy if someone is upset with me!

Do you

- Go out of your way to make absolutely certain your
  actions are approved by everyone?
- Worry for hours or even days if you hear that someone
  is dissatisfied with you?
- Lose sleep, stewing about a remark that might have
  been critical?
- Fall apart emotionally if somebody doesn't like you?
- Agree to do things you don't want to do rather than
  risk displeasing somebody?
- Say things you don't mean because you think they're
  what others want to hear?

These are signs of the people-pleaser. If you recognize
them, you may be twisting relationships by pleasing people!
Read on.

Do others

- Take advantage of you, use you, even abuse you?
- Talk about your kindness, generosity and soft-heart-
  edness when they really mean they can rip you off
  whenever they wish?

- Forget you when they're giving, remember you when they're taking?
- Give you the jobs nobody else wants because they know you won't refuse?
- Take it for granted that you *like* to be treated like a natural resource instead of a person?

These can be relationship ramifications of people-pleasing, evident in the behavior of others.

AREN'T WE ALL PEOPLE-PLEASERS?

Most readers will conclude that the label applies to them to one degree or another. And why not? Isn't every relationship nourished as we please one another? Isn't the person who deliberately affronts others, goes out of his way to displease, and conducts relationships like an extermination program just a sick sociopath or a hopeless megalomaniac? Isn't nearly everybody a people-pleaser? Doesn't *God* want us to consider what pleases others and act accordingly?

How do we separate "normal" from "abnormal" people-pleasing? How can you know if your willingness to please others is the sort that twists relationships? The line must be drawn by the Word of God. The Scriptures deal with the issue of people-pleasing. And while we are encouraged to give considerable thought to what is noble in the sight of all (Rom. 12:17, RSV), we are strongly discouraged from using what pleases man rather than what pleases God as the standard and norm for our actions (Eph. 6:6).

Let's draw conclusions. It's fine, even desirable, to please others. But when our desire to please man draws us out of the will of God for our lives, it has gone too far. Then it will twist, first of all our relationship with God, and in addition it will twist our relationships with others. It is a twist in your relationship if

- you find yourself cancelling God's plans so you can do what pleases a human being;

- pleasing others causes you to lie or commit other sin;
- you have to "fake it," put up a front, pretend and hide the way you really *are* to please someone;
- you're miserable about failing to please, more worried about displeasing man than consoled because you've pleased God;
- pleasing others is so important you're usually feeling guilty because somebody else is displeased;
- you're known as a "pushover," a "soft touch," a "patsy" because you don't dare say no or do anything anyone might not like;
- you aren't in touch with your own feelings because you're so good at conforming to whatever is expected of you;
- you feel controlled by others much of the time because they know how to push your guilt buttons and determine your behavior.

Perhaps you'll remember Trevor. We introduced him in an earlier chapter as the man who, though grown up and married, still took orders from his mother and obeyed her to the letter. A potentially successful businessman, Trevor's inability to displease people had led to several nearly disastrous business decisions. People-pleasers like Trevor have a pathological aversion to saying no. It's hard to think of a more effective way to ruin a business!

John, a pastor, like many in his profession, was sensitive, intuitive, and empathetic where others were concerned. He saw others as good, and yearned for good relationships with everyone. His desperate need to please made him a sitting duck for exploitation. People called him unnecessarily on holidays or at 3 a.m. and never heard a word of rebuke or displeasure. All of this appeared gloriously self-sacrificing. But John's family paid a price for his compliance. They suffered deprivation and neglect. John's other *significant* relationships fell apart, so he had no real friends. All due to the misguided willingness of this man to be exploited by one and all.

Brian, a skilled salesman, complained to his counselor about how he had no feelings—didn't think he even loved his wife or his children. He didn't have much reaction to the fact that they had left him and his marriage was evidently shipwrecked. This thirty-eight-year-old man had always practiced what psychologists call *denial, repression, and intellectualization*. That is, he dealt with anything emotional by assigning it to a part of himself with which he was out of touch—a sort of storage bin he never opened.

From what has been said, can you discern the reasons for Brian's peculiar alienation from himself? He had practiced such people-pleasing that he had even learned how to not entertain feelings others wouldn't like! Instead of feeling, Brian "reasoned" and "explained" the rightness and wrongness of everything. This inner twist had snarled up two marriages.

Margaret was a woman who *never* got angry. She fell apart, however, if anyone showed anger toward her. To this depressed young woman, God revealed a part of herself she had never known. Even though she was forty-two, the part of her that was still a child believed a hypothesis she had constructed before age ten.

Living with a parent whose anger frequently erupted into loud shouting and furniture-smashing, Margaret, terrified and helpless, assumed she would be smashed like the broken chairs if she ever showed anger. So she tried to stave off these episodes of terror by pleasing the fractious parent, and especially by forcing herself to feel no wrath. Result: Margaret saw herself with all the backbone of a creampuff, hated what she saw, and felt the pain of it. Worse, other people noticed her panic at the very notion of conflict, took her for a creampuff, and proceeded to use her—a twist she despaired of understanding until, in response to prayer, the Lord began His revealing work.

Brent kept everything running smoothly wherever he was. He never did anything to make waves. He hated it when anyone else made waves—even on an important matter.

Brent would do whatever he could to restore calm to office or home. When his wife showed impatience with their son for forgetting to feed the dog, Brent took it as a personal failure and fed the dog himself. He thought of himself as a peacemaker, never noticed he was a people-pleaser, and couldn't figure out why he hadn't made his home happy. Hadn't Jesus promised happiness to the peacemaker?

If your story resembles one of these, you need to notice that people-pleasing has gone too far, twisting your relationships with God and others.

TWO COMMON TRAITS OF PEOPLE-PLEASERS EVERYWHERE

Though nuances vary, people-pleasers will recognize themselves by the presence of certain traits common to all.

Primarily, you are operating by the use of *indirect, passive-aggressive behavior.* You can't be very direct if your most pressing personal need is to please others. So you will rarely indulge in straightforward communication. Sentences you avoid like the plague are those beginning with such words as "I want you to . . . ," "I would like you to stop . . . ," "I don't like . . . ," "I would appreciate it if you would . . . ," "No, I don't want to . . . ," or "Will you please . . . ?"

Instead, you will look for excuses and rationalizations. You will prefer explaining to the other person why a course of action is reasonable over simply admitting you'd like him to do it. Preferred sentence starters: "I can't do that with you because . . ." (here you come up with the best excuse you can muster); "It would be best if we didn't do that because . . ." (You give reasons rather than simply stating that you don't want to); "You should do that because . . ." (rather than declaring that you want the other person to do it).

When it comes to dealing with anger, you really tangle things up! You try to hide it, but something inside you won't let it die, so it comes out in subtle ways that surprise even you. Your indirect anger is so contorted that the other person doesn't know why he feels like he's been clobbered, and you can't understand it either. You may even be at your sweetest when you are doing the clobbering!

THE PEOPLE-PLEASER'S MISBELIEFS

Why do people-pleasers do what they do? What drives them to such anxiety over others' reactions? What makes them willing to stake everything—even God's favor—on making others happy with them?

If you are a people-pleaser, you probably account for it to yourself by saying you have a low self-concept or poor self-image. Or maybe you just tell yourself you're the *nicest* person you know without trying to explain your marvelousness.

Perhaps you've reminded yourself that in some ways you're quite successful socially and that people usually like you. "Look at all the friends I have," you think. "I must be doing something right!" Maybe you notice only occasionally what it's costing you to be so well thought of, or that few of the many people around you seem very close. Perhaps you shake off your concern by thinking, "I'm too busy to get in so deep with anybody."

The fact is people-pleasing behavior grows out of a *radical misbelief* you developed long ago in the context of your primary relationships. You haven't yet corrected the childish thinking you developed so many years ago. Here it is:

If I don't please everybody with everything I do, someone may become angry at me or dislike me. I would then feel guilty, and that would be dreadful!

Do you believe that? If you do, you will do your best to please. And you will endorse the corollaries:

- It's essential for me that everybody love me all the time.
- I must keep everything smooth and see that nobody makes waves ever, anywhere, about anything.

- I mustn't get angry, mustn't show anger, mustn't let anyone else get angry.
- I mustn't have any feelings that are unacceptable to anyone.
- I'd better agree.
- I should wait for others to initiate, be passive, stay out of trouble.
- I mustn't argue.
- I couldn't stand losing love (anybody's, for any reason).
- It's vital for me to be charming.

If God is revealing that you hold beliefs like these and, as a result, you have twisted important relationships, you can choose a new path leading to restoration and renewal.

REQUIRING AND RESTORING FOR PEOPLE-PLEASERS

In the case of people-pleasers, God's initial requirement involves strange and unusual activity, for many in this group have systematically avoided thinking about their inner lives since childhood. That is, they have practiced repression, denial and intellectualization as substitutes for honesty in appraising their own truest thoughts and feelings. A prerequisite for restoration of twisted, damaged relationships in this group is to learn the habit of *thinking*—straightforward, deliberate and systematic review of their own relationship beliefs.

If you are serious about change, we recommend that you keep a journal. As you live each day, log your interactions with others, particularly those with whom you have twisted relationships. Keep track of your conversations and actions, *and ponder the self-talk underlying these behaviors.* Most important of all, log what you tell yourself about these interaction episodes with others, making sure to capture the nuances in your thought.

Notice when you get upset over human interactions. Note the event about which you made yourself feel hurt or angry.

Then write it in your journal, as well. Next, describe your emotional reaction and how weak or intense it is. Third, write out what you are telling yourself about the event, your internal monologue. As you write, underline the misbeliefs you find in your self-talk, noticing when those listed in this chapter pop up. It's important to catch misbeliefs as soon as you can after they run through your mind, or even better, while you are telling them to yourself.

Give careful and deep thought to recalling your first relationships. How did you learn, in their context, to think that you must always make sure, *at all costs,* to please everybody? Reconstruct the story for yourself, recognizing that, at some point, you devised your theory about how to get along. And from that theory your radical relationship misbelief about people-pleasing developed. Write this out in detail in your journal. Careful attention to this step will go a long way toward convincing you that your misbelief is childish thinking, and that, as an adult, mature in Christ, you don't have to cling to it anymore.

But don't stop there! God has revealed all this to you, and is requiring that you challenge your misbeliefs energetically, and just as forcefully replace them with the truth. Now write out your challenge and the new truth replacing old, childish misbeliefs.

NEW BELIEFS FOR FORMER PEOPLE-PLEASERS

Begin to look at yourself as a *former* people-pleaser who has now become a *God-pleaser.* And tell yourself the truth:

I don't enjoy having people upset or angry with me, but I might have to tolerate such things, because my choices won't always please everybody, and sometimes they may please nobody but Jesus!

Moreover:

I can stand it if someone is upset with me, is angry with me, or chooses not to like or love me.

I don't have to have everybody's love; I don't even have to have anybody's love except the love of Jesus.

Others have to solve their own problems; I can't keep everything smooth for everybody.

Sometimes, when I am rightfully angry over something important, I need to show it even if someone doesn't approve.

It's no disaster if I've made someone mad; they can get over it.

My feelings are my feelings; if I have them I have them, whether anyone else likes them or not.

Sometimes I need to disagree or argue with someone, even if they don't like it.

It's legitimate for me to say no, or, I want you to, or, I don't like . . . and to use other direct expressions.

ACTIONS LEADING TOWARD CHANGE

Give some thought to behavior you can try which will convince you that you can survive without necessarily aiming always to please others. For example:

- Once each day, tell someone honestly one of your actual feelings, even if it is negative.
- Every day, try arguing with someone (argument is not hostile, uncivilized, or unholy—argument is making as good a case as you can for your point of view). Practice making direct requests of others, especially try asking someone to change some behavior.
- Practice refusing the requests of others, but only when you feel sure God wants you to do something else. Practice saying no without offering excuses.
- Study Psalm 18, and make notes in your journal to demonstrate to yourself that you need the love and friendship of God, and that, having that, you can survive and even be happy, even if others disapprove of you for some reason.

THE NEW "YOU"

What will the new person be like in whom God is doing His work of restoring relationships?

To begin with, let's hope you don't cast aside all those excellent social skills you learned as a people-pleaser. Those pleasant, agreeable ways will always stand you in good stead. You know how to show honor to others by consideration, courtesy and politeness. You are probably able to put them at ease. You have very likely developed skills of talking with others about *their* concerns, listening attentively while they express themselves, and demonstrating the ability to put your own concerns in perspective as you gain understanding of the interests of others.

You need only add the freedom conferred by the truth, to stand firm when it's not necessary to act pleasant and agreeable.

So, although you will be a giving, empathetic, soft-hearted, loving person with many friends, you will find yourself going deeper and becoming more intimate with some *because you are now able to share your inner self,* taking the risks involved in intimacy that we discussed in Chapter 5.

And you will find yourself free to express such reactions as disapproval, irritation, anger, or disagreement without fear of loss of love or rejection. You will discover that if someone does withdraw love for a time, hoping to manipulate you or load you with guilt, you will survive just fine. You will refresh yourself at the fount of God's love in Jesus Christ, discovering what many others have found—that it's the only love you absolutely must have for survival.

So, the new you will be more relaxed, less conflicted, less tense, less fearful and worried. And, accordingly, your old, guilt-laden, people-pleasing, twisted relationships will be renewed and restored.

NINE

The Controllers

Few of us *want* to be known as controlling, overpowering people. Because we all have negative feelings about being controlled, we prefer not to be like those awful people who go around trying to make others over in their own image.

As we, Bill and Candy, worked jointly on this chapter, we remarked to each other, "I don't think I'm a controlling person. Do you?"

We agreed stoutly that the idea was far from the truth.

But after a thought-filled break in the conversation, Candy said softly, "You do know we both like to control situations, don't you, Bill?"

Reluctantly, Bill had to admit that we probably are controlling, to some extent.

Some of you will have settled the issue before God long ago. They readily admit knowing that they desire overmuch to control nearly every relationship. "I'm chagrined about it," you might add, "and it does make relationship difficulties for me. I want to work on change."

Others will now examine themselves for the first time for an unbiased self-assessment. Without flinching, ask yourself, "Am I a controller? Am I ready to work on change?"

WHAT IS A CONTROLLER LIKE?

Let's have a closer look at the traits that accompany the habit of controlling other people.

Most controllers are unaware of their tendency.

When an instance of controlling so blatant it can't be ignored comes to their attention, they may chuckle at the notion that they have the habit of running others' lives. They say, "Oh yes, I suppose I am just a teensy weensy bit liable to take charge of things. It's just the way we *able* people have to be, you know. It's our burden in life!"

Typically, they rationalize: "If I didn't make sure things run smoothly, who would?" Or, "He won't do it, so I *have* to— otherwise it wouldn't get done." Or, "She just can't think ahead. It's a good thing *somebody* uses the brain God gave!" They call their controlling by another name—a label with a more virtuous ring to it, like *prudence, caring, only making a suggestion,* or *sheer necessity* ("I *had* to say . . ."). They tell you they are only planning ahead, getting organized and taking adequate forethought (when others, of course, are not). They see themselves as hard-working ants in a world of grasshoppers.

Many maintain their lack of insight by controlling so *indirectly* that even they can't see what they're up to. Often the person being controlled is slow to catch on, too.

For instance, you may leave a book lying around open to a passage you want someone else to read (and obey). Maybe you push someone to attend a church service where you think the preacher's message will say what *you* want your friend to hear (and obey). Or you formulate questions so the controllee practically *has* to condemn himself out of his own mouth for what he "should" be doing but isn't. ("And what did you do next? Go on, tell me! What do you think you *should have done* at that point? That's right, admit it!")

Another indirect tactic: questions meant as thinly veiled commands. "Are you going to get that dishwasher repaired today?" "Have you called the phone company yet about our bill?" "What are you going to do about the leak in the garage roof?"

Some anxious people are true artists at using their *anxiety* to control other people. A new client told one of us,

"Please don't tell me anything that's even a tiny bit negative because I get upset. Then I won't be able to sleep tonight!" Anxious spouses have been known to train their mates to accompany them docilely to every appointment and even to the grocery store, because both believe the anxiety that might otherwise follow would be too awful to tolerate.

Then there are devices intended to arouse *guilt* and thus motivate the subject to action. "It must be nice for you to go bowling with the guys. I've been taking care of these kids without a break for over three weeks!" "I'm certainly rushed in the morning, what with making my own breakfast. I guess you're pretty tired in the morning and need to sleep in, don't you?" Jean Jacques Clemence (in Camus' *The Fall*) habitually confessed his own guilty history to strangers so they would tell him of the skeletons in their closets—a special source of satisfaction to Clemence.

Sometimes controlling people even *change* in order to get someone else to change. Wife changes churches to get husband to go with her. One roommate cleans the apartment as a hint to get the other to make his bed.

Dropping verbal hints; trying to be funny when you're actually very serious about wanting someone to change; falling silent so conspicuously that the other person notices and tries to discover why; crying without explanation until the controllee begs and grovels to find out what his fault might be; being late to let the other know you can't accept his behavior; dampening your mood just enough to signal to someone that she's not quite making you happy; putting the candy in a cupboard because you don't want her eating any more of it; arranging the seating so *he* can't sit by *her* because you know they're not good for each other—the possibilities for indirect control are endless if you're a good finagler.

Controlling people, though they are sometimes pushy, authoritarian, dictatorial souls with no subtlety or artfulness, most often come off more skillfully as cute and sweet, or humorously, cleverly persuasive. For those who feel frightened of life's challenges unless they have a controller to depend on, skilled controllers make it difficult to resist. In fact, when they're really artisans, you can hardly even guess what they're up to. So, lacking insight into their own real game, and surrounded by people who can't understand the rules either, controllers are often dumbfounded and resistant when someone tough points out what's happening.

That's why we're doing our best to persuade you not to jump to the facile conclusion that you never control anybody. Some of the most accomplished controllers we know have insisted on precisely that point. So neither the controlled one or the controller can understand the undercurrent of dissatisfaction, unrest and unexplained hostility he senses in others. Yet this undercurrent can be a still, small voice, guiding to the discovery of truth and the real untwisting of a twisted control relationship.

BEING CONTROLLED

It's not as hard as you think to be controlled by someone. Many of us *let* ourselves be controlled. We've been taught that it's nice to go along with the suggestions of others, to cooperate, to agree. And it's not very nice to refuse, balk, resist, or say no.

If it happens that you are a push-over who lets yourself be controlled in an important relationship, you must learn to discern and put a stop to the controlling person's domination *for your own sake, for the other person's good, and for the sake of your relationship.*

Stop telling yourself you're only being submissive and truly Christian when you let yourself be controlled like a horse with a bit in its mouth. To see true submission, look at Jesus. Did anyone control Him? No way! He even said of His trial and crucifixion, "No one takes [my life] from me, but I lay it down of my own accord" (John 10:18). His perfect submission to the will of the Father kept Him free of the domination of those who would gladly have taken Him by force to serve their private purposes.

INSIDE THE CONTROLLER

Anxiety. If you are a controller, you most likely have certain traits in common with other controlling people. For instance, the way you feel deep inside. No matter how smooth and polished or rough and bossy you may appear on the surface, deep within lies a lump of anxiety. Controlling people not only want their way (who doesn't want that?), they believe they must control everything in order to avoid discomfort. They control so they won't have to worry.

If you are a controller, you worry about dire consequences if a matter takes its own natural course, if others are allowed to make decisions and choices without direction, and if you have failed to manipulate events toward what you *know* must be the proper outcome. Others won't find it easy to shoot down your worries with platitudes. Most controllers have practiced arguing their case until they have themselves convinced. Very likely you can reel off a number of sad catastrophes that occurred when you let someone else run things. For each occasion, controllers remember clearly the logical and historical progression from the moment when they lost control to the eventual terrible outcome of past events. They recall these events as warnings to themselves in case they ever come close to letting down and giving matters to God or anybody else to take care of. As a controlling person, you are truly convinced you must control or things will be terrible.

Alienation. No matter how chummy you may appear and how much time you spend with other people, you feel isolated and alone. The word alienated contains the word alien, i.e., one who belongs elsewhere. That feeling, that you belong somewhere else than with those around you, is caused by your conviction that you are the only one who can run things adequately. How can you welcome closeness to others when what you truly believe makes you separate and different from them?

Furthermore, even if your controls are applied subtly, others eventually catch on to the truth. And since no one wants to see himself as anyone else's patsy, even the people-pleasers eventually get tired of your need to dominate them and separate themselves from you. Since no one is really able to breach your walls of controlling and achieve closeness with you, they give up and move away and you feel even more alienation.

Depression. You cannot have two mutually exclusive things at once. Your need for companionship presses powerfully for fulfillment, and at the same time, your overwhelming compulsion to dominate others pushes them away from you. Your frustration must persist until you give up one or the other goal, since you cannot have both. That frustration may be apparent to you only as a perpetual inner sadness, painful, but not severe enough to merit the clinical diagnosis of depression.

Controlling people can become clinically depressed when someone important moves out of their lives.

Sometimes indirect controllers use depression, suicide gestures, or even actual suicide to manipulate someone else. The object may be guilt, compliance, or love. Because suicide threats can be powerful motivators, such manipulators usually get their way—for a while. When at last the dominated one kicks over the traces and rebels against such unfair control tactics, the controller might make a really lethal suicide attempt: a sad, final, ultimate control tactic. If you are a suicide threatener, you *must* get help toward the goal of freeing yourself from the awful burden of having to force and dominate others. You are the one who will appreciate the freedom most.

Perfectionistic. "Don't do anything if you can't do it right" might be taken as a motto by many controlling persons. Ask yourself if you are a perfectionist. As has been explained elsewhere, the biblical goal of perfection set forth by Jesus serves as an end point toward which every person should strive. Your problem, if you're a perfectionist, is your belief that any result short of perfection is so unutterably disgraceful that you should never try anything unless the outcome can be guaranteed perfect.

Controllers know others will make mistakes. You may think, pridefully, that others are more likely to make mistakes than you. And in your anxiety about outcomes and over-inflated certainty of the rightness of your own techniques, you try to make sure by either doing *for* others things others should do for themselves, or by coaching, guiding, directing and advising so as to prevent others from any possibility of "error." To make matters worse in this regard, it is often (not always) true that the controlling person *can* deliver on the promise of the song from *Annie Get Your Gun*: "Anything you can do, I can do better!" Maybe you can. But that doesn't mean you always *should*.

Compulsive. You might pride yourself on your impeccable neatness. Orderly to a fault, many controlling people drive other people crazy with their refusal to tolerate mess or muss in their bailiwick for even a limited time or even under exceptional circumstances.

Just when someone is trying to make a sandwich in the kitchen, you might elect to clean the top of the refrigerator (and while you're at it, the door and the inside too). Many a football-watching husband has been irritated to distraction by the vacuum cleaner running under his chair just at the game's moment of truth. Perhaps you are the hostess who firmly (but carefully) throws your house guest's blow drier in her room. Of course you told her the guest bathroom was hers during her stay, but you didn't mean she could leave it messy because you "just can't stand" having things lying around.

Do you often feel that somehow others must be forced to embrace, endure and imitate your nit-picking neatness or you can't be happy?

Critical. We realize how difficult it is to admit to criticiz-

ing others, even when you've just finished correcting someone. Extreme honesty and rigorous self-appraisal are therefore crucial if you are to grasp the truth that you are a
critical person. Controllers habitually find fault with others
and tell them about it, sometimes with meticulous detail. It's
hard to accept that you are a faultfinder.

Perhaps it will help to pay attention to what others say
about you. Do you sometimes think others find you disagreeable? A comic character in Gilbert and Sullivan's opera,
Princess Ida, is so sure his criticizing is for the benefit of
others that he can't think why people say he's disagreeable.
Maybe you'll see some of your own characteristics reflected
with kindly humor in his patter song:

> If you give me your attention, I will tell you what I am!
> I'm a genuine philanthropist—all other kinds are sham.
> Each little fault of temper and each social ill effect
> In my erring fellow creatures, I endeavour to correct.
> To all their little weaknesses I open people's eyes;
> And little plans to snub the self-sufficient I devise;
> I love my fellow creatures—I do all the good I can—
> Yet everybody says I'm such a disagreeable man!
> And I can't think why![1]

Manipulative. Of course, nobody can control others without manipulating. Many people fail to distinguish between
manipulating and requesting. There's nothing wrong with
asking someone straightforwardly to do something. That's
not manipulation, and it's totally legitimate (as long as you
aren't applying indirect pressure at the same time). Manipulation is not merely requesting change. It is *underhanded*
control by artful, unfair, or insidious means. Very often, manipulation is indirect. Sometimes it is direct, but unfair or
even aggressive.

"*Super-spiritual.*" We'd better make clear what we mean
by this term. We *don't* mean positive, genuine spiritual life.
We're thinking of a phony spirituality with which some con-

---

[1]Copyrighted, Decca Record Company Limited, London. Exclusive U.S. Agents,
London Records Inc., New York 1, N.Y.

trollers impress themselves and a few others. If you are a super-spiritual controller, it is possible that no words from us will get through to you. You are too well defended with self-righteousness. You live on the illusion that your plane of holiness is so far above others that it's only natural and right you should be in control. You believe you exist for advising, helping, directing, and even guilting folks into following the path you've laid out.

What is saddest is that, all along, you will act such a marvelously convincing role that you will pull the wool over your own eyes! You may deceive *some* people, but mostly you deceive yourself. You surround yourself with those you have deceived so no one who isn't taken in by you can tell you the truth. Your personal needs are gratified by keeping several of these overdependent "leeches" clinging to you and your false spirituality. If, for a time, there happen to be no leeches in your life, you may feel unsure of your righteousness and that makes you uncomfortable.

You talk special holy language so you don't sound like others who are not spiritual enough to suit you. You preface virtually all your observations with "God told me . . ." because your leeches will take the words that follow more seriously if you do. Your prayers for others are patronizing and condescending, and you cannot imagine any petition for them better than that they become just like you.

Only one route to insight can be open to the *super-spiritual,* and that is the convicting power of the Holy Spirit. Unfortunately, you can build the wall of your religious defenses high enough to bar entrance even to Him.

You *can* get help. If God allows you to see yourself, even dimly, as *super-spiritual,* find a wise counselor who knows how to confront and lay bare for you the misbeliefs with which you support your hypocrisy, and how to minister the truth that can set you free.

If you suspect that you may be the person we're describing, pray for God's revealing work to begin. He can come through the hardest of defenses if you want Him to, and He can rescue you and your fake relationships too no matter how far down this road you have traveled.

ISN'T CONTROLLING JUST NATURAL FOR PEOPLE?

Why do we want to control other people? Is the urge natural? Normal? Do all living beings have it? All humans? All sinners? Some men, half-joking, insist the trait correlates with femaleness, while some women insist it is man's nature to want to run things.

Let's make some distinctions. The pathological desire to control is different from merely asking someone to change a behavior *for reasons of our own.*

To illustrate: Sol couldn't keep employees in his store because he hung over them, observed every move they made, and chattered an unbroken monologue ("No, no, not that way . . . this way"; or "Here, let me show you!"). He had a warped desire to control everything.

Chad, another store owner, let his employees know what he expected them to do, unhesitatingly communicated his needs and corrected what he saw as undesirable behavior. His employees, for the most part, stayed on to work at his store. Why? Because Chad didn't continue to direct people who had learned to do what he wished. Nor did he feel uncomfortable leaving his employees to carry out their duties without his watching their every act.

Sol, the controller, exhibited abnormal, pathological urges to force others into his mold, ignoring *their* need for freedom and a degree of self-determination. Chad had learned not to be ashamed to make requests of others directly and pleasantly. We can all think of people like Sol, controllers because of their anxiety about every outcome over which they don't have complete charge. And we have known others who, like Chad, had no hesitation about asking for what they wanted without manipulation, put-downs, or indications that they desired to run every detail of everything. Our feelings can help us. To the Sols, we react with aversion, and our feelings urge us to escape from their gimlet eyes. To the Chads, we generally react with relaxed good humor, feeling free to make choices, knowing they won't be upset if they aren't determining everything for us.

We conclude: It's normal and constructive to make requests of others openly and frankly when we need to. It is abnormal, destructive for relationships, and even sinful to believe we must determine others' choices and actions (and sometimes even their feelings) for them. Because we are all sinners, many of us will find occasional tendencies to engage in controlling behavior. The damage to our relationships may be the first sign by which we become aware of how deeply our flesh and our ancient Enemy, the devil, have deceived us.

RELATIONSHIP TWISTS AND RADICAL MISBELIEFS OF CONTROLLERS

Controlling people damage their relationships, causing pain by the twists they produce. Although pain is generally felt first by the controlled, it will come to the controller eventually. And though the anguish may be severe for you as the controller, embrace it as it forces you to give heed to what you might never notice otherwise. You are injuring your relationships and damaging yourself. Pray for insight and for God's work of revealing. As you discover your radical misbeliefs, the pain will carry out its divine mandate.

If you listen to your self-talk, you will discover that you act as you do because of underlying misbeliefs. Controllers rehearse their notions to themselves, in some cases almost constantly. These internal verbal stimuli elicit the controlling responses we have described.

GUILTY GEORGE'S RADICAL MISBELIEF

The burden of having to operate the universe had twisted George's relationships with everyone. At the end of the line,

George even twisted his relationship with his own body. This resulted in ulcers, sleeplessness and constant nervousness. George had driven others away until he was left to operate the whole cosmos by himself.

The pathological need to be in charge followed from the radical relationship misbelief George invented at age five when his mother died.

George had been close to his mother. One day, not long before her death, he became angry, as children will, over one of his mother's disciplinary tactics. He was furious, frustrated and unforgiving for a few days. Suddenly, unexpectedly, his mother fell sick and died. His father could not pull himself together and was hospitalized for depression. The little boy, suddenly alone, cared for by some distant relative, brooded over his losses. Out of the blue, he thought he realized why all the bad things had happened to him. Totally unaware that the idea was nonsense, George decided *he* had caused his mother's death. He, George, was responsible for the fates of the others.

He now saw himself as a powerful, important, guilty person. His anger had killed his mother and put his father in the hospital. How vital it was to be careful and control *everything* and *everybody*.

Here is George's radical misbelief. Many controllers share it. We can label it *controllers' radical relationship misbelief #1*:

> *Unless I control everything, things are "out of control," and then something awful will probably happen that would be my fault.*

WHAT MANIPULATING MIKE TOLD HIMSELF

Manipulated spouses react in different ways. Some knuckle under and meekly allow themselves to be controlled without complaint or resistance. Slowly, insidiously, they drift away from the marital relationship and center their lives elsewhere: career, hobby, sports, friends. They may simply escape into their own world of alcohol, drugs, or even indiscriminate TV watching. They never rebel openly; instead, they simply shut the controlling one out of their lives. The relationship has twisted until it exists only as a formality.

Separation or divorce may be the path reluctantly chosen by the manipulated one in a controlling marriage relationship. Although relationships twisted past this point rarely untwist, God can and does bring them to life when both people are willing. Whether such marriage renewal happens or not, it is singularly important for anyone whose marriage has destroyed itself to take on the painful task of self-examination. You must face the question: Are you a pathological controller? If you don't make changes, you will twist relationships yet to come.

Still others stay in the relationship and fight back, becoming more hostile and complaining as the years go on. These marriages become less and less attractive to the observer, and others avoid these bickering, crabby, rancid twosomes because of their unpleasantness. Eventually, facial expressions become almost frozen into permanent expressions of resentment and dissatisfaction. Sadly twisted, those relationships! Are you in one because of your own controlling? It's not too late to seek God's revealing work now with the aim of untwisting your relationships.

Manipulating Mike lined up the lives of his family members (and friends, where he could) as if they were chessmen on a game board. He liked to make all the moves, determining who, what, when and why on behalf of others. What they wore, whom they befriended and dated, where they went, what they planned for the future, and nearly everything else had been Mike's to decide until at last the family fell apart. Compulsive, perfectionistic, overly neat, and above all *prideful*, Mike's field of vision had been so crowded directing the affairs of others that he neglected to examine his own behavior. He couldn't see himself as others saw him. When, after the separation, even the kids pulled away, Mike's pain finally stabbed deep enough to force him to consider his controlling.

When Mike finally let the hurt turn his gaze inward, God could reveal, require, and restore.

Mike's radical relationship misbelief would have to come to light. Learned in childhood from his prideful father, who believed it word-for-word as Mike had come to believe it, this deeply ingrained falsehood creates trouble in many families. Here is what Mike thought was the case. *Controllers' radical relationship misbelief #2*:

> *In order for me to feel comfortable and safe, every detail of others' lives must correspond with my visions for them. If they don't, they won't turn out for the perfect best and that would be downright tragic.*

ALIENATED ANITA

Controllers have trouble with their children, especially after they become adults.

Anita, for example, had hardly noticed the emptiness while Jeff was alive, for she had kept busy managing him. Now he was gone. Alone in her vacant nest, Anita stewed. Why did the children almost never call anymore, never come to visit her? *Ungrateful,* she called them in her heart. They would have explained their behavior differently.

Twists caused by manipulative parents distort their relationships with offspring for years after the young have moved from the home. The controller may never learn what's wrong because children reared by controlling parents think it's useless to try to tell them.

Anita's parents were positive, outgoing, successful people. They lived well, practiced their Christian faith wholeheartedly and loved their children. The entire family had appeared exceptionally attractive, and they were held up as a model home by many. You couldn't have found *anything* wrong with them. Anita couldn't either. She grew up believing so in her perfect family that her faith in God drifted into second place. She knew only that she had to make herself and her entire family conform to the perfect model of her childhood home.

All her life, poor Anita believed the *controllers' radical relationship misbelief #3*:

> *My parents were perfect, and because of that they were always right and always successful. My worth depends on being as right and successful in everything as they were, so I have to be perfect and make my children perfect too.*

"SUPER-SPIRITUAL" SUE

You would never have guessed that Sue spent whole days at home in bed, thoroughly dosed with prescription medications meant to ease the strains of life. She carefully hid all that from everyone outside her home. Nobody must know how terrible was the toll of her frustration with those unwilling to receive her spiritual insights. Occasionally, her depression became so bad she stayed in bed from one Sunday to the next, getting up only to teach her Bible class. No, you wouldn't have guessed, because Sue appeared strong.

A leader in her church, Sue was so "super-spiritual" that many feared to approach her, since they could never measure up to her high level of refined understanding of things spiritual. She maintained an indispensable coterie of followers to help her guide, direct and order others' lives, but none of them even dreamed of reaching Sue's elevated heights. And then there were those who seemed to Sue inappropriately unimpressed. She found it a continual frustration that others would not ascend the heights to which she sought to call them. She often felt sure within herself that she had "the Word of the Lord" for her pastor and the church council, as well as for various others. No one dreamed how intense was her irritation at those who did not dance to her tune. She ascribed her negative feelings toward those who would not become her puppets "spiritual concern" for them. She believed it herself, though at times this "concern" made her nearly homicidal.

Though her childhood had been full of baubles and toys, Sue had never had sufficient control over everyone else to make her truly happy. Though her every whim had been indulged by passive, people-pleasing parents, Sue's satisfactions, such as they were, came from being in charge. Even as a toddler, Sue told her parents and others how to conduct themselves. Occasionally, she commanded a guest to vacate a chair she had determined was "for Mommy." People generally did what she told them to, so Sue learned to think life was meant to go that way. She developed her own erroneous theory about how relationships ought to be, formulating for herself *controllers' radical misbelief #4*:

> *Since people in power do what I want them to, I must be superior; since I am superior, people should do what I want them to, and when they don't my life has lost all meaning.*

Sue also came to believe that

> *Being superior means being spiritually superior; that I am, and people ought to recognize it.*

and

> *Since I am so superior and super-spiritual, I quite naturally have an inside track with God; others absolutely must recognize this and obey us (God and me).*

Acting on such notions, Sue created a situation in which genuine friendship was impossible for her—with God or man. No wonder she experienced such despair. How will the Lord find a way to reveal to Sue what the problem is? And when He does, will she accuse even Him of not being sufficiently spiritual?

ANXIOUS ANNETTE

Annette's anxiety attacks resulted directly from her belief that terrible responsibility rested on her shoulders. She positively had to handle so much. She couldn't imagine what would happen to the affairs of others if she didn't "help" them all with her advice. It all seemed so overwhelming. She doubted her ability to handle such burdens, but never once wavered in her conviction that she "should" direct one and all. In response to such notions, Annette's autonomic nervous system kept her revved up. No wonder she felt overanxious at times.

When Annette was ten, her parents finally ended a dragged-out separation, which had stretched over five years. During all that time, neither of them did a thing to bring about resolution of their conflicts, but both kept encouraging little Annette to hope. The child, believing as children do that *she* had to help, tried every tactic she could think of to bring her parents together.

When her father remarried, Annette began to experience attacks of panic. Clearly, according to Annette's belief system, she had failed because she should have tried harder. Nothing she thought she could count on was certain. Only her very best efforts to make things work out might from now on be sufficient to keep her world intact. The child never connected what she heard about Jesus and her heavenly Father with the notions about meaning that she was formulating. At some point in this process, Annette developed her hypothesis, which later hardened into the misbelief governing most of her later relationships. We'll call it *controllers' radical relationship misbelief #5*:

> *The foundations of my life are shaky. There is no one I can trust to stabilize or hold things in place but myself. I'm not sure I can do it but I have to try because I can't handle another relationship earthquake like the loss of my family. I must manage the affairs of my loved ones.*

In Annette's case, anxiety provided an alarm bell to call attention to her erroneous interpretations of relationship reality.

- Are there warning bells in your life?
- Do people reject you after a relationship gets going? Have you been utterly stumped trying to figure out why?
- Are your family relationships strained, hurtful?
- Do others start retaliating for something you can't imagine you've done?
- Have you been ignoring the hints friends have dropped about your attempts to control them?

Pain connected with relationships, even major setbacks like loss of friends or divorce, may be a vital clue that something is wrong with your behavior, attitudes, and relationship beliefs.[2]

How will you react? Your response to emotional pain can make all the difference to your future. Research findings have indicated that among people who have suffered heart attacks, those who blamed the attack on others or on stresses outside their own skin had a higher rate of second attacks and death. Those who saw the sickness as an occasion for changing their beliefs, spiritual values, understandings and relationships had a lower rate of second attacks and death. Take the opportunity to find out whether you need to change.

THE TRUTH IS . . .

Replacing the controllers' misbeliefs with truth can make you a new person.

Here, in outline, is the truth about matters of controlling: In place of the misbeliefs that now lead you to panic until

---

[2]Not always. We are *not* among those who assert, dogmatically, that it always takes two to ruin a relationship. If you are involved in a painful loss situation, get help from friends who will tell you the truth. It may be entirely due to the other person's problems. We are only suggesting that relationship losses *may* signal a need to assess the degree to which you are a controller.

you insist on controlling everything and everybody, learn to insist on these facts:

- *I will survive if someone else decides*
    or chooses
    or carries out the program.
- *It can fail, he or she can fail, even I can fail, without the world coming to an end.*
- *If I don't decide, choose, or do it, it may not be done as well, but I can handle that.*[3]
- *I don't have to stay in this bondage; for freedom Christ has made us free; I can walk in freedom if I choose to.*

If you will accept your emotional and interpersonal relationship troubles as occasions for turning to the Lord for His threefold work—if you will get serious about change as He *requires,* and honestly look at yourself that He may *reveal* truths in place of old misbeliefs, He will *restore* a life of wholeness in relationships to you. But if you *blame* others, and insist that circumstances and God are at fault, insisting that you simply must run everything, you will hang on to your misbeliefs and suffer their miserable consequences for your relationships.

HOW TO CHANGE: WHAT GOD REQUIRES OF CONTROLLERS

Step 1: Start a journal.

Although we can't claim some divine decree for journal-keeping, we *do* advocate journaling because we consistently have found it to be a powerful change device. If you purpose to change, and haven't done so already, start a journal. Record, day by day, your experiences and the changes you find

---

[3]What if you are responsible for the outcome, as in the situation where you are the boss and an employee does sloppy work? Obviously, you are appropriately in charge and expected to see to it that the careless worker improves. When it is appropriate because of authority relationships, you are expected to direct some of the behavior of others.

occurring. Use your journal to work systematically on your misbeliefs.

Step 2: Relinquish.

As you read, in Christian literature, about the necessity of "turning everything over to the Lord" and "releasing others to God," you may puzzle over how you're supposed to do that. Where's the manual of directions you need to assemble your new "release kit"?

Good question. You'll find that, like assembling your new ping-pong table, it's a process, not a one-step operation. Most people get as far as the beginning, but it's only a beginning: prayer. Though prayer by no means is the entire process, you can't go on until you've begun. So tell God: "I'm sick of controlling _____. I'm taking my hands off the steering wheel. You drive. The situation is yours! Amen." There's something indispensable about that solemn declaration before God, made with the realization that God is listening, and even more spine-tingling, taking you up on your commitment! He'll require that you come through with the goods, but He'll also come to your aid with His truth, His resources and His power.

Just like that, relinquish. Relinquish everybody and everything that you've been scared *not* to control. Now it will be God's responsibility to run things and to handle directing people.

Have you made this beginning? You've just told God He has your permission to be God! You've just put God back in the place where He belongs and resigned from trying to take His spot as Lord of the universe. Just think, you can put the world down off your shoulders if you like. You can quit worrying!

Note the date and the content of your prayer in your journal. It's a momentous event. Treat it as a milestone.

Step 3: Resolve to be open and honest.

Now resolve before God that you're going to quit kidding yourself. You're going to quit lulling yourself off to sleep thinking how much others really need your chairmanship over their lives. You're all through pretending to yourself that you have a superior wisdom such that you alone are fitted to operate the control panel for just about everything. You're going to pay attention to the swollen size of your ego, the magnitude of your pride and the height of your self-exaltation—all required for you to keep chucking yourself under the chin, smiling and telling yourself you're a wonderful and necessary controlling person.

Tell God, in addition, that you purpose to take a new stance of openness before Him, before yourself and before others. Psychological defenses have good purposes when they are employed properly. But when you become so defensive that you're blind to your own impact on your relationships, you're too well defended. That's one way to fall prey to the deceptions of the devil. Ask God to fill your mind with the Holy Spirit of Truth. Screw up your courage to risk being guided by Him to view the unvarnished facts about yourself and your habitual role in twisted relationships. Much as you don't want to, you must see your controlling operations for what they are.

Being honest also involves admitting to others what a controller you've been. Here is some scriptural help toward openness with God and others:

> Search me, O God, and know my heart; try me and know my anxious thoughts; and see if there be any hurtful way in me, and lead me in the everlasting way (Ps. 139:23, 24).

Make this psalm your prayer, offering openness to God: "*Search* me, *know* me, *try* me, *see* me, and *lead* me"! That says it all.

When you announce solemnly to God that honesty is your purpose, you have established a baseline for your new behavior. You can check yourself against it daily. So write your resolve into your journal.

Step 4: Be controlled yourself by another!
Here is a word about controlling that rockets the entire discussion to a much higher level with eternal significance.

For the love of Christ controls us, having concluded this, that one died for all, therefore all died; and He died for all, that they who live should *no longer live for themselves,* but for *Him* who died and rose again on their behalf.

Therefore from now on we recognize no man according to the flesh; even though we have known Christ according to the flesh, yet now we know Him thus no longer.

Therefore if any man is in Christ, he is a new creature; the old things passed away; behold, new things have come. (2 Cor. 5:14–17)

From the above, attend to these facts:

In relinquishing control I have come to be *controlled.* The love of Christ controls me.

Peace will take the place of my old, inner striving as I tell myself the truth about who is in control.

This requires living, not for self, not only for others, but for the gracious Lord, who suffered and died for me and rose again in triumph over the deceiving, misbelief-generating Enemy on my behalf. The Enemy's deceptions cannot hold me any longer.

By the power of the risen Christ whom I know as my Controller, *I am new!* The old need to control has passed away, behold, the new has come.

I now have no need whatsoever to control others, for I and they are controlled by Christ.

Step 5: Record your relationship self-talk to find and change your misbeliefs.

In your journal, take pains to record every impulse to control other people and/or circumstances (and note whether you did or did not carry out the urge to run things). Jot down the words of the monologue running through your head at the time. Examine your jottings to locate and write out your misbeliefs. Challenge those erroneous thoughts as God reveals them on the page in front of you, and write out the challenge and the truth.

Here is a sample journal entry for a controlling log:

Journal-Controlling

Date	Impulse to control Did/Didn't	Internal Monologue & Misbeliefs	Challenge & Truth
Sunday Aug. 7	Thought of banging around so Martin would wake up and go to church with me. I could get him to church without being pushy by just "accidentally" making enough noise to wake him up. Didn't do it— made journal entry instead.	He really should get up for church, you know. He didn't go last week either. He's getting in the habit of oversleeping. You should make some noise. Once he's awake, he'll go. He needs you to give him just a little shove to improve his Christian walk. Misbeliefs: I have to make sure Martin does right. If I don't, he won't. He needs me to do that. Things never work out properly if I don't see that they do. No telling how awful that man would become if I didn't nudge a little here and there.	Who made you Martin's conscience? He's a grown man whom God requires to take responsibility for his own decisons, including whether to sleep or get up for things. You're telling yourself you have to make yourself important to Martin by "improving" him, and you're telling yourself you can avoid being a bad controller by being indirect. It's your old childhood hypothesis that if you don't make everybody in the family do right, it'll be a disaster because they'll all blow it. Not true. Let Martin do wrong if he chooses. God doesn't kick him out of bed. Why should you?

CHANGING YOUR WAYS

Although working with your log on developing new, truthful beliefs and self-talk about your relationships is the centerpiece of your efforts to give up controlling, you can make some other changes, too. All of these will help improve relationships damaged by past efforts at control:

First, change the way you talk to other people. Replace

hinting, questioning, guilt-producing, and other indirect methods of communicating your wishes with truthful, open communication. (You can get help from the book, *Telling Each Other the Truth*, by William Backus.)

Second, learn the art of listening to others. One of the most ingrained habits of controllers keeps them attentive to their own thoughts, ideas and programs *even when others are talking to them*. They may hear enough so they can respond, but not enough to actually understand emotionally. Most often controllers listen to God as poorly as they listen to people. It is loving to listen carefully and to struggle to understand other people.

Here are the activities you can learn to perform to be a good, loving, "truthful" hearer: *attending, active reasoning, creative empathizing, intuiting, letting the Spirit enlighten, facilitating, giving feedback.* You can learn more about the skills of listening by studying Chapter 9 of the book referred to above, *Telling Each Other the Truth*.

Third, practice delegating tasks you've erroneously convinced yourself only you can do. Record your delegating in your journal and write down how it worked. Was the task done reasonably well, even though you let someone else handle it? Did you make yourself uncomfortable over the issue? Did you log your misbeliefs and replace them with truth?

Fourth, practice saying new phrases to other people. After you say them, mean them and stick to them. Don't offer others the chance to make decisions and then take it back when they make a decision you don't care for. Try to find a way *at least once a day* to say things like:

- "It's your decision. I'll go along with whatever you decide." Follow through by replacing your own misbeliefs with truth.
- "You choose what movie we'll see this time!"
- "What do you think?"
- "Why don't you give me your thinking on the issue?"
- "Lord, on this issue, not my will but yours be done!"
- "I have no plans for our day (or week or vacation or

whatever . . .). I wanted your ideas!"
- "Why ask me? Wear whatever you like."

Remember, you'll have to really allow the other to make decisions and choices. It's not enough just to say words. In the process, you'll have to deal effectively with the misbeliefs you'll encounter in your internal monologue. Use your log. And be sure to make journal entries about your changed behavior as well as how it's working to improve your relationships.

SPECIAL STRENGTHS OF CHANGED CONTROLLERS

There are strong points and assets in everything God has made, including controllers. When the Spirit of Truth accomplishes His changing work in them, their strengths can emerge.

The desire to control others can be softened in some until it becomes a positive quality, giving rise to special gifts of leadership. You may have particular personal qualities developed over years of habitual planning and directing for others that are not bad in themselves. God can make use of them once He has cleansed the misbeliefs out of your self-talk and calmed the worrying that springs from mistrust of the ability of God and others to handle things. Very often people who have a problem with the need to control also have excellent characteristics waiting to be used.

For instance, such people may be especially:

Responsible. If, in your controlling modes, you have been over-responsible for concerns appropriate to others and to God, you may find you are, in the non-controlling mode, an exceptionally responsible person. What a positive trait this is in a world where psychopathic traits seem almost glorified and people are downright proud of their sloppy irresponsibility!

Perceptive. Often, you will find yourself able to see the whole scope of an issue, scan its process from start to finish, and sum up the whole for others who are not able to capture wholes as you do. Perhaps you are a quick thinker, so that others who want and seek your help (not having your wisdom foisted on them) will benefit enormously.

Organized, planful, prudent, making appropriate provision for what's ahead. There is a sense in which it is true that people with such gifts are ants in a world of grasshoppers. When these gifts are brought under the control of the Holy Spirit and informed by the truth rather than misbeliefs, they can be a tremendous asset, not only for self, but for others—when they want your help (not when you merely assume they need it).

Good leaders, directors, managers, committee chairmen. When others have no need to resist *your* efforts to control them, *they* will seek you out. For quite often controlling people have underlying expertise fitting them for leadership positions. It may be necessary for you to do battle always against the tendency to return to your internal monologue with its old, destructive, anxious beliefs that pressure you to try to control. If you are successful, allowing the Spirit to replace pride with humility, you will find great satisfaction in leading, delegating and assisting others in arriving at goals *they* wish to achieve.

So don't conclude that you are a hopeless controller who will always go on alienating others, putting them on the defensive and feeling miserable unless you are pushing others around! Fix your aim on the positive qualities we've pointed out. These are precious traits you can be given by God if you seek His will and, in accord with His love, determine to change your relationships by changing yourself!

TEN

So How Can I Untwist My Relationships?

How can you have untwisted relationships?

The quick answer to the question is, *untwist yourself*!

Because we humans are such infinitely creative beings, we have discovered an incredibly large number of ways to twist our relationships. We have presented a few selected examples to illustrate the principles in untangling knots. Here are a few more common relationship twisters.

THE PASSIVE PERSON

Passive people often attract controllers, since they appear to make ideal controllees. Ask them to make a decision? They rarely do. Instead, they throw it back into your lap. But the catch is, you can't win by making decisions for them! They dislike decisions made by others, and resist even when others choose at their behest. This leaves their friends and loved ones in consternation and confusion.

Who's going to initiate, move, execute, determine, choose and act? Not the passive person. He waits for another to do it. He then goes along, saying he *has* to, but resents *having* to. This resentment he will express passively, not overtly and directly, but by stubborn resistance or noncooperation.

If you are a passive person, you probably know your astounding ability to confuse others by your indirect backlash. They hear you say one thing and do another when you resent and resist the decisions they make for you after you've told them to do so.

Glenda, a passive young woman, keeps her marriage in chaos by demanding, with Bible in hand, that her husband exercise headship. When he does, Glenda becomes indirectly aggressive and takes revenge by forgetting, wheedling, or quietly and unobtrusively doing the very opposite of what she knows her husband wishes. All this time, Glenda, like other passive persons, appears wonderfully pleasant, cooperative, positive, sweet and compliant.

The passive person twists relationships by getting others to work at pleasing them. They keep raising the hoop for others to jump through. Usually, the other will try for a while, but will finally give up in frustration.

Often, passive people were rewarded in childhood for being shy, never making trouble, being "seen and not heard." Their parents may even have discouraged active, decisive, or choice-making behavior. It's logical to hide your feelings and keep quiet if you are ridiculed or blamed for showing strong personality traits, or for trying to cope on your own.

Tommy's father discouraged his son's attempts to help himself. The boy's coping efforts were met with responses like, "Oh no, Tommy, let me do that. You can't handle it. Tommy, that's a wonderful picture you drew. What is it? Oh, a tree. Well, well. Here, let me draw a tree for you—the right way. What are you trying to do? Dust the living room table? Oh no, you might knock over the figurines. Here, let me."

Once, Tommy determined to surprise his father by mowing the lawn. The mower stopped running, Tommy couldn't get it restarted, and Dad lost his temper. He punished the entire family by refusing to speak to anyone. Tommy's mother cried. Tommy concluded, "All this is my fault. I shouldn't have tried it. Nothing I try works. I can't do anything. It's so terrible to try and fail, I'm better off waiting for others to do things. I suppose I'm not talented. I'm probably going to fail at whatever I attempt."

Tommy hammered out this hypothesis to explain his life situation. Here is his radical misbelief, the same one held by many passive people:

> *People blow up at me because I try things; I can't do things as well as others, so I'd better not take a chance on trying. Better to wait. It's terrible if I fail.*

Can you, if you are a passive person, recall some interactions in your own primary relationships where you formulated your radical relationship misbelief? The light of truth sometimes flashes on when a person notices how distorted his childish theories were about what was happening to him.

Here's the truth. Failure is not terrible. Only avoidance can do you in! Not trying is the cardinal sin for you if you are a passive person. You have spent years practicing avoidance because you believe you can't learn, can't succeed and shouldn't try. Now is the time to recognize that your first efforts may not exhibit great skill and accomplishment. So what? Give yourself credit for making those efforts. If you fail, accept failure as part of life and learning.

Passivity can also be found in people-pleasers.

THE POOR LITTLE PERSON

These people present themselves as needy, helpless and inadequate. They may especially attract *Big Mama* or *Big Daddy* types. Often, though they are fully grown adults, they picture themselves as young, small and immature. Soon after becoming involved in relationships that provide opportunity for it, they become emotionally dependent. This dependency knows no bounds, for these people behave as if they are bottomless pits of neediness. There is never, in any relationship, enough to satisfy their needs. No matter what is done for them by others, they want and expect more. Their warrant for such seemingly exaggerated expectations is their perpetual pitiful plight. So, poor little persons attach themselves to others like leeches.

Soon the other discovers he doesn't have the resources to sustain the poor little person. But, how dismaying! The p.l.p. won't take hints, can't hear the word no, and won't go away, even for a break. Typically, p.l.p.'s insist it is the other's moral obligation to give them first aid, bind up their emotional wounds, and be available to them whenever they want nurture. They expect friends to be mother, daddy, or nurse to them even though they are adults.

Poor little persons can demonstrate great ingenuity and energy, not in solving their problems, but in manipulating others to do it for them, in locating others who have tried to hide from them and in arguing their absolute right to be taken care of.

Others become weary and drained. They develop a painful conflict between the sense of obligation elicited by their friend's "need" and their own desire for relief from the demands. Eventually they pry the poor little person loose and kill the relationship. If you are such a poor little person, you will have had your heart broken more than once in this way.

Since they'd met at a church singles' gathering, Marlin's sticky dependency on Jan had increasingly fastened him to her. At first, Jan encouraged him. Something about his air of naivete and helplessness appealed to her need to be needed. She felt special and good as Marlin sought her listening ear and motherly advice. So she assured him that his middle-of-the-night phone calls were no problem. After all, she knew how hard it was to have nobody to turn to. And Marlin did calm down nearly every time she prayed with him. It was miraculous how his anxiety subsided. Marlin's requests for Jan's time and her listening ear multiplied. She told herself Christian love demanded she be available, open, unconditionally positive. And she stifled her irritation, scolding herself for finding Christian love so difficult.

The negative feelings snowballed, however, and at last, Jan asked Marlin to stop leaning on her.

He explained that he could not stop. He needed her help too much. He felt suicidal. He increased the intensity and number of his demands. He saw no excuse for Jan's failure to be available. He saw himself as a poor little person, weak, helpless and needy. Hadn't he been taught that the only Christian response for Jan to consider was 100 percent availability?

If you are someone like Marlin, will you take this opportunity to reverse this fatal twist in your relationship life? Can you see, from the story of Marlin and Jan, how imperative it is to stop blaming others now and pray and work toward insight and change?

THE RADICAL MISBELIEF OF THE POOR LITTLE PERSON

If you are the poor little person, here is your own radical misbelief:

> *Others owe me succor, time, energy, caring and a bottomless reserve of love. I am entitled to all this because I am such a little thing, clearly unable to cope myself; therefore others owe it to me to take care of things for me.*

If you have been playing this role, now is the time to examine the origin of your radical misbelief. See if you can recall childhood events in primary relationships where you fabricated explanations or hypotheses about the meaning of those events. Spell out how you may have guessed at the reasons for things. Can you now, as an older person, discover the origins of your early radical relationship misbelief?

The truth? You have no letter in your hand signed by God guaranteeing the boundless care and concern of other people! Only God's love, care, concern, interest and attention are boundless, unlimited and unconditional! Other people are weak, sinful, fallible, limited human beings like you. Your helplessness is an illusion. As long as you believe the lie that you are paralyzed, you'll never get up and walk. Break your habit of hanging on others: It's your drug. Nobody owes you a single thing that you are perfectly capable of providing for yourself. In fact, one of the major lessons you must learn is that relationships are reciprocal—two-way streets—in which both persons find their own needs met. They are not one-way alleys down which others must travel to meet you and fulfill your wants.

BIG MAMA/BIG DADDY

These folks try to look and act superadequate, more than equal to all challenges. They may show obvious hostility toward anyone they perceive as a competitor. But they are tender, kindly and nurturing to poor little persons. Big Mama/Big Daddy persons try to satisfy their social needs by surrounding themselves with p.l.p.'s toward whom they assume the role of a parent. They even try to manipulate other acquaintances into assuming a needy stance. They seem to be saying, "Tell me your troubles and I will try to help." They pick up on anything another person does to suggest need for counsel. They're always ready to advise. They feel good only when they are helping, and the sole basis on which they can relate is their own superiority. The only way for them to feel superior is to eliminate that dratted competition from other adequate persons and to surround themselves with p.l.p.'s who gladly accept their subordinate role—the price for having dependency needs gratified by Big Mama/Big Daddy.

Jan, the harassed "victim" of poor little person, Marlin, was actually not a victim! At least, not in the beginning. Jan unconsciously sought to encourage dependency in others, and whenever she met someone like Marlin, all Jan's relationship misbeliefs poured into her self-talk. She virtually offered Marlin a shoulder to cry on, a strong pillar to lean on and an inexhaustible storehouse to draw from. For Jan's desire to feel important, meaningful and worthwhile—

normal wants, to be sure—had long been channeled by her misbeliefs into relationships with others.

Only later on in some of these relationships did Jan rue them, wondering how such people always attached themselves to her, and upsetting herself with conflicting self-talk engendering hostility and guilt. Like most Big Mama/Big Daddy people, Jan made no connection between her relationship failures and her own behavior and misbeliefs.

If you are like Jan, you need to change because you cannot have closeness, equality, mutuality, or exchange of openness in your relationships. Because you must always be the counselor, you cannot know the happy contentment in a relationship of mutuality. Many people of this type become professional psychologists, psychiatrists, social workers, pastors, counselors. They cannot drop their professional masks even when they are socializing.

Here is the Big Mama/Big Daddy radical misbelief:

> *I am not valuable unless I am superior. I can never compete with equals, so I need inadequate, poor little persons to keep signalling to me how big, powerful, valuable, influential, important, and helpful I am.*

Perhaps, if you're a Big Mama or Big Daddy, you can ponder some of your early relationship experiences, discover your early interpretations or hypotheses, and thus uncover the theorizing you did when you first formulated your radical misbelief.

The truth? You can and must find ways to limit your helping behavior by recognizing and communicating that you are only a finite creature, not the infinite God you've been pretending to be. Tell yourself you must interact with people who don't need help, no matter how uncomfortable you may be with such persons right now. Tell yourself you can survive without always feeling powerful, big and important. Tell yourself you can observe and imitate the social behavior of others who are not always playing Big Mama/Big Daddy.

GENERAL PRINCIPLES FOR UNTWISTING RELATIONSHIPS

Many readers will have found themselves in one of the examples we have given. If you have not found yourself described exactly, you can still apply the principles for untwisting twisted relationships. Here is a summary:

First, pray and give thanks daily for your twisted relationships, for the others' needs, concerns and interests, and for the untwisting of your personal twists. *Pray on the basis of God's promise to do the work of revealing, requiring, and restoring.*

Second, practice love and kindness. Show concern for and interest in others. Let others know of your desire for their company and the happiness you feel with them.

Third, develop firmness and toughness. Relationships are not fostered by your treating the other person as though *you* have no interests, needs, desires, or concerns. Yes, theirs are important, but so are yours. It is up to you to let your reasonable expectations be known. You can feel good about your toughness only if you believe firmly that the other person's good is not served by letting him or her abuse you. Forgiveness is not the same thing as allowing another person to mistreat you whenever he wishes.

Fourth, practice direct communication, including speaking up, saying no, making requests and listening. Practice self-revelation and encourage the other to do so, too.

Fifth, *know yourself.*

If you have read this book with an open heart and mind, comparing yourself with the examples, you may have learned some things about yourself. You should also study your relationships, examining them for untwistable twists. Ask others for input about your relationships. This may seem difficult, but it can be appropriate at the right time and place to ask another, "How do you see our relationship? How do you see the part I'm playing in it?"

Especially, determine your relationship misbeliefs. Do this by:

- keeping a journal—a terrific means by which God can reveal your misbeliefs to you—a great way to *know yourself*;
- paying close attention to your self-talk in relationships;
- logging your self-talk in tight relationship spots;
- noting and writing out your misbeliefs;
- detecting and challenging the errors, the false assumptions and the downright lies of the devil you discover in your misbeliefs;
- writing out the truth of the matter, i.e., how an impartial and objective observer might see it; how God might see it.

Find your radical relationship misbeliefs by recalling your early primary relationships. Did someone tell you in so many words the untruths that now form those misbeliefs? Can you remember some important person modeling the misbelief for you? Can you remember traumatic episodes where you invented a hypothesis to explain the facts? Can you remember listening to the devil, the world and the flesh so that you came to erroneous conclusions which hardened into your radical relationship misbelief? When you recall the genesis of your misbelief, and see for yourself how it arose out of childish thinking,

- tell yourself the new truth in your life situations; and alter your actions in relationships to accord with the new truth you've begun telling yourself.

Keep trying. Change may come rapidly for some. For most people, changing self is difficult, slow, time-consuming work. And changing relationships can be even more exacting because another's behavior must be included in the equation. Even if the other person won't meet you halfway in your attempts to change, consider each personal improvement a victory because your new relationship behavior will improve at least some of your relationships and may help you form new ones.

HOW TO BEHAVE IN A GOOD RELATIONSHIP

Now, to summarize, we detail some of the qualities a person needs to develop to enjoy *good, untwisted* relationships.

Truthful self-talk. Don't wallow in the self-talk of discouragement when you find relationship twists. Don't tell yourself you don't need relationships, or devalue the relationship you are having trouble with. Don't grumble, "Who needs other people, anyway?" The answer is—*you do.*

Take an open stance toward your own faults, and to the possibility that you have caused some of the twisting. When the other person tells you your faults, accept the correction by acknowledging its truthfulness and changing your behavior when appropriate.

Remember the principle of mutuality. Do not expect the other to do all the pursuing, all the contributing, all the giving, all the considering, all the discerning. Don't demand perfection of the other while making allowances for yourself. Relationships are a two-way street.

Cultivate goodness. This admonition appears trite and our impulse is to answer, "Of course, goodness! What else? The point we're making is that good people make good relationships. Practice behaving according to the highest standards set forth in God's commandments. Don't let yourself off the hook just because you think you might get away with some sinful behavior.

By the same token, search for good people with whom to form relationships. Granted, at first, some evil flaunted by others may seem tantalizing and exciting. Relationships with bad people might temporarily appear spicy. But, in the long run, a good person will want to form relationships with good people because such relationships offer positive benefits rather than future trouble and only such relationships endure beyond temporary pleasure or profit.

Seek the good of the other person. This may require a change from thinking of nothing but what others can do for you. Don't forget, too, to seek relationships with those who desire and sincerely will your good. This stance of desiring the other's good and actively pursuing it is the love of Christ. It is here contrasted with the love that seeks its own fulfillment, although that love, too, has a place in relationships.

Spend time and effort with the other person, making your contribution to the relationship. Why should you expect relationships to drop into your lap or to take care of themselves? The prevalence of this erroneous expectation may explain why so few golden relationships exist.

Give the relationship time to develop. Don't expect instant closeness, instant intimacy, or instant "credit" (e.g., "Now that we've been friends for a couple of weeks, I know I can borrow his car, ask for money, or request his time purely for pursuit of my interests.") A relationship is slow business, it has ups and downs, and when cultivated properly, it grows over months and years.

Begin each day by exercising your relationship with God through Jesus Christ. Most of what has been said applies to this relationship. Take time to talk things over, to be with God in silence, to pray and praise, to hear Him speak to you in the Word, to be sensitive to His wishes, to trust Him for good, and to do what pleases Him. This relationship can become the scaffold for your other relationships.

Are you discouraged with relationships? We find so many people, especially young people, who have decided, prematurely, that they can't ever have good relationships. They've tried, things haven't gone well, their relationships got twisted, so they believe they *can't* have untwisted relationships with family or friends.

Don't be discouraged. Put into practice the teachings of the Scriptures. Work on personal change. Use this book to the fullest extent by doing the things suggested. If you haven't begun your journal, why not start now? If you haven't prayed deeply about your own relationships, why not do it today?

You can begin now, with God's direction, to untwist your twisted relationships!

ELEVEN

A Crash Course in Friendship

Now it's time to turn our attention to the positive! We have been absorbed in the intricate twists of human relationships and toiled hard at learning how to untwist them. Let's finish our work by stepping back a pace or two and look at what we're trying to achieve. What is good friendship like, anyway? And how is it done?

Good relationships *are* friendships. Even where there are blood ties between two people, it is when they are friends that their relationship shimmers with joy.

When a relationship has the positive quality of a friendship, we speak of that relationship as *loving*.

Loving relationships = friendships

WHY WE NEED ONE ANOTHER

God made us with a built-in need for other people.[1] His remark about how bad solitary living was for Adam (see Gen. 2:18) was not idle conversation!

Jesus, the exemplary Man, needed friends. He didn't appear on earth like a Greek god, living above the human riff-

---

[1]The word *need* here is used in a relative sense, as in *need* for food and water. Our eternal life and final well-being do not depend on such things, so we don't *need* them absolutely. In this sense, the one thing *needful* is Jesus Christ.

raff around Him, untouched, unconnected. He had kinfolk. He had students in training. He had friends. And, more intimate yet, He had companions. He was not ashamed to admit out loud that He *loved* His friends. It is from carefully observing Jesus' way of living, above all, that we can determine how good relationships can be for us.

When we are in trouble, friends are our only refuge after God himself. Friends help us to avoid making mistakes, they take care of us when needed, and do for us what we cannot do for ourselves. They prompt us to do courageous and noble acts, drawing out what is best in us.

MAKING FUN OF MOTHER-LOVE

A strong tendency in popular culture has diminished the so-called *natural virtues*. For instance, there is a prevailing tendency to demean mother-love as "mere" animal instinct. Friendship is seen as nothing but temporary convenience, and the love between parents and children is viewed as pure self-interest on both sides. Marriage for many today is very nearly a commercial arrangement in which husbands and wives sign contracts to protect their material assets. In this view of things, friends relate on grounds of convenience and usefulness, rarely professing *love* for one another. These new tendencies are pronounced "honest" instead of "hypocritical," and we learn to expect the rip-off in what's left of our relationships.

The Bible exalts friendship to a high status, praising love between relatives and friends. What God has declared good, man cannot demean without penalty. The penalty in this case is shoddy and unsatisfying connections between people.

WHY DO I LOVE YOU? LET ME COUNT THE REASONS.

Most people think they know what is *good* for them. They may also be completely wrong. The homosexual values sex with one of his own gender as *good*. By scriptural criteria, he is wrong. You may value someone's penchant for flattering you as a supreme *good*. You may also come to rue the day you committed yourself to such a friend.

Often, the *good* we look for in a relationship means qualities like pleasure in the other's company, finding fulfillment and receiving care. We usually find it *good* that another desires our companionship for no other purpose than enjoyment. We like to be desired that way by someone whose company we desire, because this makes us feel valuable. Some say we like those who are like us ("Birds of a feather flock together"). Others insist that, on the contrary, we are drawn more to those who are different from us ("Opposites attract"). Both are correct. An ideal companion might be a person who is enough like ourselves that we share a large domain of commitments, values and interests in common, but different enough to supply what we lack and provide correction, abrasion and argument where they are needed.

Among the highest goods is *goodwill*; that is, the other person wills good for us. Moral or spiritual goodness—including a grand capacity for love—is the highest of the qualities we call *good* in a friend. This kind of goodness is the quality of greathearted persons who are able to give themselves unstintingly and with no self-consciousness about their giving.

Therefore, people who love each other are good to each other and want good for one another. If you want to be a good friend, you must learn to sense what the other considers good and make an effort to provide it. In our experience, those who want relationships based on attraction and strong feelings alone will have them—but their friendships will be shallow and of short duration, since neither person invests much. People whose relationships consist only of mutual pleasure or mutual usefulness (as in play, sex, or business) will find that when one of the parties changes, pleasure and usefulness evaporate—and so does their friendship.

SO, WHAT IS PERFECT FRIENDSHIP?

One of the enduring songs Christians sing together is about the perfect friendship: *What a Friend We Have in Jesus.* If the words are boiled down to their central meaning, the song teaches that Jesus is the perfect friend because He not only wishes our highest good, but He alone unfailingly knows what good is and He is able to provide it. The song is based on Jesus' *revealing* His perfect friendship by *laying down His life for us.* (See John 15:12–17.) Offering yourself for your friends is the supreme act of willing and seeking their good.

And yet, even the perfect friendship cannot be a one-way street. When God is our Friend, He *requires* response from us. "You are my friends if you do what I command you." (See John 14.) What He commands is that we love as He did. A perfect "circle" of willing and doing good for one another would mark the perfect friendship.

Immediately, many Christians would say, "Nobody is perfect except Jesus. Therefore, all of us will fall short as friends. All human relationships will be somewhat twisted by what is bad in us." These statements may be true. Nevertheless, we want to aim at the target of perfection. To that end, let's envision for ourselves *the perfect human friendship,* for it will be modeled after the kind of friendship Jesus demonstrated.

The perfect human relationship will involve two persons who are good, for bad persons are capable only of flawed and twisted friendships. These two perfect friends will be alike in virtue, for they will truly wish each other's good. They will love one another in full and equal measure. And because of this love, they will be capable even of laying down their lives for one another.

Those who wish the good of their friends, spouses and relatives, giving themselves for the sake of the others, are friends in the truest sense. These relationships are not "here today and gone tomorrow." They do not depend on transient qualities like pleasure and usefulness, but on the goodness of the characters of the persons involved. They will therefore endure eternally because true goodness is an eternal quality. These relationships will offer the most pleasure and usefulness of all (though pleasure and usefulness are not their object), for good people are helpful to one another. They are pleasant to one another, too, because they are pleasant in themselves. Everyone finds pleasure in doing what he was designed and created to do (praising God and loving one's neighbors). So all good people find real pleasure in the actions and interactions of true friendship.

Some human relationships come close to this picture— ideal-sounding as it is—though it's true that friendships approaching perfection are very uncommon. If you find one, you have found a treasure! Yet all of us can work at building relationships founded on the good and lasting qualities Jesus showed toward us.

TIME

Such golden relationships are not quick and easy to build. They require time, hours and days spent together in situations both good and bad. We must also develop that quality of simple familiarity. For as the old saying has it, "You don't really know someone until you've eaten a pound of salt together." (Do you know how long it would take to eat a pound of salt?) Friendship is slow business.

So is the business of untangling relationships that are twisted.

As you go to work on these relationships, enter first and fully into the perfect relationship, the friendship that *is* eternal life: I'm speaking of that deep, rich fellowship with God and with His Son, given by His Spirit. This friendship is open to you now.

If you have never begun this friendship with God, I urge you to do it now. Confess your sins to God. Invite His Spirit to give you a new birth. Tell Jesus you believe in Him and trust Him as your Savior, your Lord and your one flawless Friend. Then keep your eye on this perfect relationship as you work through this book to untangle your other relationships. Use your friendship with Jesus as a model. But refrain from discouraging and upsetting yourself because you never quite reach perfection. Perfection*ism* can kill you and your friendships!

As you participate in this divine relationship by faith, prayer and Scripture reading, God can use the material in this book to do His work of *revealing, requiring and restoring* what is needed to take the twists out of your human relationships.